About this book

Have you ever looked at your cat and wondered: what are you thinking? Or questioned why they have a habit of running around the house in the middle of the night? Maybe you've even considered training them in an attempt to stop misbehaviour but believed it impossible.

What if I told you it wasn't? What it all comes down to is: understanding cat behaviour!

Cats are well known for being difficult to understand, but in fact, their behaviour is fairly easy to read once you take a moment to learn why they do what they do. What this book aims to teach you is exactly that!

We'll cover everything from how cats interact with their human companions and other cats, to how to read and interpret their body language and vocalizations, and even how to train your cat. And yes, they are in fact trainable!

Cats are eccentric and independent animals, but that doesn't mean they're impossible to understand. If you want to get to know your cat better, learning more about their behaviour will help! Not only will it foster closeness with your kitty, but you will gain the ability to provide them with an even happier and healthier home. Want to know more? Pounce into this catastic guide on the inner workings of our feline friends!

Cat Behaviour & Language

Learning cat sounds, what they like & effective training for a happier feline friend

M Ellis

By Morgan Ellis

By reading this document, the reader agrees that under no circumstances is the author responsible for any losses, direct or indirect, that are incurred as a result of the use of the information contained within this document, including, but not limited to, errors, omissions, or inaccuracies.

Table of Contents

Introduction

Cats are notorious for being eccentric and mysterious animals. The way they express affection is even contrary to how humans have come to expect; Consequently, many people tend toward brushing them off as uncaring or unloving.

There are countless jokes and memes in which cat insults are the punchline, but a lot of these stereotypes are simply untrue. Sure, cats aren't overly expressive, but they feel a wide range of emotions such as love and your need for companionship with them. Understanding your cat from this perspective comes down to studying its behaviour, just as any other animal or person. Like humans, these creatures have layers.

One of the most intriguing facts about cats is that they tend to have personal tastes concerning a wide variety of things. Preferred food and water, smells, and even toys can vary between them. So not only do cats have diversified personalities they also have distinct preferences. Spending time with and getting to know your cat, apart from being enjoyable, is also an excellent bonding experience.

The best way to understand cat behaviour is to get a good insight into how they interact with us. How this differs or remains the same when around people, compared to other animals or on their own, illuminates the inner workings of a cat's mind and emotions. The fact they change some behaviours in our presence also conveys an attempt to communicate with us directly—albeit obscurely.

Additionally, by learning how a cat's brain works and perceives the world around it, we can understand its motivations. We frequently are prone to assigning human emotions, ideals, and thoughts to animals or even inanimate objects. But most animals do not see things the way we do: both literally and figuratively; Cats are a prime example of that. Taking a moment to comprehend their point of view can help you see things from their unique vantage point. In doing so, making wiser decisions concerning your cat will be a breeze.

Now, when it comes to discussing the behaviour of cats, there's a lot of ground to cover. The various vocalizations paired with general body language will typically convey their feelings when applied as direct communication. On the other hand, habits—kneading, hunting, pouncing, and even grooming—have a standard of sorts. Recognizing this clue will allude to the potential physical, mental, and emotional problems of your companion.

Further, cats rely heavily on their sense of smell, perhaps even more so than any other sense. Not only can it distinguish whose territory is whose, but also glean information about other felines and even warn of potential toxicity! Getting to know just how their noses work, as well as what smells they like and dislike, can be incredibly beneficial in multiple ways. A good grasp of this feature will help you to create a safe and comfortable environment for your kitty.

In addition, they are fairly territorial by nature. Even cats kept indoors their entire lives still have a marked domain they live within and protect. Ever wondered why they shepherd you around the house and defend invisible boundaries within it? Discovering the significance of their definition of territory can clue you into these habits. Moreover, issues within the home may heavily influence mood and impact their health. The good news is, keeping their environment safe, stable, and healthy will be that much easier with the knowledge found in this book!

We all know eating, drinking, and even sleeping are pivotal to the survival and wellbeing of humans; Naturally, cats are no different. However, despite the similarities between the base criteria of human and feline habits, a cat's tendencies are rather different from ours. How frequently they eat, the amount of water, and hours of sleep necessary, all play a primary part in their wellbeing. For that reason, this book will aid you in developing the ability to discern the difference between normal and potentially concerning daily habits.

Besides the ability to charm food out of us, your cat might possess an uncanny knack for getting into trouble. Whether they decide to scratch up your couch, pounce on your feet, or make a habit of climbing onto shelves to knock everything onto the floor, our cats are known to be frustrating. But contrary to popular belief, training is possible! Time and patience are all you really need—along with a few successful training methods—and you happen to be in luck! Chapter nine has all the techniques to get you started ASAP!

Last but not least, the social dynamics of cats are particularly important. When planning a multi-cat home or other pet addition, such as a dog, it's not as simple as adding a new critter into the mix and hoping it all works out. This process entails recognizing mannerisms around other animals, which is essential for even solo kitty homes. This is due in part to the fact these habits often mirror interactions with their owner and others.

By and large, the amount of information concerning cat behaviour is vast. It may even seem a bit overwhelming. But not to worry! In this book, we'll break down the numerous aspects in detailed easy to read sections. Once you start learning, their once absurd habits will begin to make perfect sense. Understanding the influence behind these actions will not only positively impact your perceptions of your cat but improve the relationship you have with this beloved companion. So what are you waiting for? Grab your furry friend and let's jump right in!

Chapter 1: Human-Feline Relationships

When it comes to owning a cat and beginning to recognise its behaviour, you should first look at how cats tend to interact with humans in general. They are incredibly independent by nature and don't even need us to survive and thrive. So then why do we keep them as companions? Do cats get benefits from being domesticated? In short, yes. They gain several bonuses from living in a house rather than the wild. These include secure access to food, no longer being subject to the elements or the dangers of predators, and the tendency to live much longer (especially those with health concerns). Their owners gain plenty of benefits as well. Studies have shown a strong connection with your pet is known to alleviate some health conditions and ease stress and anxiety. That aside, if they don't *need* us, does that mean they still want us around? This may be a difficult question to answer, especially when just looking to your cat for a sign. Cats are notorious for being aloof and seemingly lacking the emotions we expect from other pets, such as dogs. But, the best way to understand the relationship trends with humans is to start at their domestication.

Cats came into domestication in a very cat-like way—on their own accord. That's right! They essentially began the process on themselves. Despite this occurring in more than one location, modern domestic cats all seem to share identical ancestors from which they evolved: The North

African or Southwest Asian wildcat. Although numerous mysteries surrounding cats and the reason for their domestication remain, studies of their DNA can at least determine where and roughly when it transpired. Such work located the birthplace of this phenomenon to lie within the Fertile Crescent. This discovery approximated the date of occurrence to be 10,000–12,000 years ago. Researchers have also noted an increase in domestication within ancient Egypt around 3,600–4,000 years ago. This research has helped to determine how domestic cats managed to spread all across the world! For instance, many cats were brought into port cities and taken along on ships. Likely to help combat rodent problems, this action allowed the spread into other areas and countries.

Another fascinating anomaly found during this research has to do with cat coat patterns. It seems that some of the genes responsible for determining this did not begin surfacing until around the Medieval period. This information suggests that any selective breeding done was initiated a *significant* amount of time after domestication began. Not only that, but this genetic selection appeared singularly focused on coat colours and patterns. There is even some evidence that suggests the colour of their fur influences their personality. However, the existence of many other variables challenges this theory. Selective breeding was also less focused on behaviour. As a result, the domestic cats of today remain significantly in touch with their natural wild inclinations.

So how exactly did cats accomplish domesticating themselves? As human villages and civilizations began to crop up around the Fertile Crescent, there was a pronounced increase in food supplies. The storage of surplus food led to a rise in the mouse population of the area. The belief is that this new prey source attracted the attention of the local wild cats. Those that hunted the mice were tolerated and allowed in the villages (rather than brought in for this benefit). The assumption is villagers kept them around due to a number of their physical features and personality traits: Their smaller size, energy level, playful nature, and degree of intelligence were all likely contributing factors. This 'domestication' thus became more of a 'taming' process: Little took place to change any aspect of their natural behaviour. So ironically, wild cats chose themselves as the best candidates and selected their most desired traits, leading to a future of life with humans.

The takeaway from this is that cats choose to be domesticated. We didn't pluck them up and start selectively breeding them to use their natural behaviours for our benefit. In many ways, this mirrors the common behaviours that cats exhibit when interacting with human companions today. They prefer to be the ones to initiate and may even get grumpy or upset if approached first. So yes, maybe cats don't need us around, but instead, they want us and even enjoy our company.

Recognising Humans

Because of how subtle cats are with their expressions and emotions, some owners may come to question if their pets even realize who they are. You know, apart from being the thing that always gives them food and showers them with affection when wanted. To answer your potential question, yes, your cat does recognise you! But it may not be in a very visual manner. See, cats don't have exceptional eyesight, and viewing objects too close or too far away is difficult. As a result, they are at a disadvantage when relying on their eyes alone. One particular study found cats make distinctions between other cats or even locations when given images as reference. In contrast, when it came to their human companions, they had more trouble picking them out from a group of strangers.

But thankfully, for our sake and our kitties, they don't have to rely on eyes alone when recognising us. Even if their optics aren't the best, cats do have other fairly sharp senses. One such is their sense of smell. Cats' noses are extraordinary and can recognise and understand all sorts of scents within their environment alone. That also includes the ability to discern you. Some studies have shown cats can recognise the voice of their owners as well. So maybe differentiating specific features is impossible, but they can tell who their humans are thanks to familiarity with their smell and voice.

So, if they can physically recognise their humans, does that mean cats can tell what emotions they are feeling as well? To an extent, yes, they seem to understand what we're feeling and can tell if it is more positive or negative. Over time they learn to associate positive body language, such as smiling and laughter, with good situations: Negative gestures they view as a lack of such. Cats have even been known to look to their owners for cues judging new and strange things in their environment. They essentially look for reassurance before approaching what would otherwise cause them anxiety. If we react positively, they are more inclined to investigate. This behaviour is called social referencing.

This type of relationship and interaction typically gets built over time. The longer someone has owned and spent time with a cat, the more a feline associates their body language with certain feelings. Cats who see you as a stranger will not have the same connection. However, you may find that your cat doesn't necessarily relate your emotions, particularly the negative ones, with a need for comfort. Cats tend to determine how your feelings affect their own needs and desires. They essentially associate your positive emotions with the positive things they acquire, such as attention, being pat, or receiving cat treats. Your negative emotions—you guessed it—become linked with a lack of these things.

How Do Cats View Humans?

If cats can recognise us and understand our emotions to an extent, then exactly how do they see us: Are we a friend or part of the family to them? Or do they think of us as beneath them and only there to give them food and clean their litter boxes?

Knowing how they view you is grounded in understanding basic cat behaviour. When cats are around human companions, especially ones they trust, they tend to display a lot of confidence and affectionate body language. For example, your cat may rub against your leg and weave in between your feet whenever you come home from work. This display is a very positive sign; Your cat is trying to greet you in a friendly manner. This action is also similar to how they would greet another cat. You may even find your cat kneading their paws against you or grooming you, despite you not exactly having fur for them to clean. Both behaviours are often exchanged between cats and are a sign of comfort and companionship from your kitty.

Much of this behaviour and the general way our cats interact with us mirrors how they socialize with their species. Therefore, it is safe to assume that they see us more as one of them and less as another species or outside entity. To cats, we are just other cats. Big and clumsy but cats nonetheless.

So, if they see us as other cats, they must see us as inferior cats, right? After all, they expect food and affection from us! While rather a common belief, it's not entirely true. There's a running joke in popular media that cats act as if people worship them. Due to their free-spirited nature and perplexing emotions, some even assume they are unhappy around us. Indeed, they don't jump about wagging tails to convey enthusiasm the way dogs do; But when near human companions, cats do feel excitement or joy. Sure, they are more independent than other pets, not the most expressive about showing feelings, and can become irritable when called (mainly when it benefits them in some way: such as being summoned for dinner, treats, or playtime), but none of these mean cats view us as subservient to them.

Understanding this is, once again, grounded in recognizing the behaviour of your cat. Those affectionate ways they greet you (or rest on you)—such as rubbing against your legs or kneading—are not etiquette shown to inferior cats. This friendly demeanor is far more akin to that used around cats who are their equals. In short, they greet us and associate with us in the same way they would a cat viewed as a friend.

Chapter 2: Understanding How Cat Brains Work

To better appreciate the general behaviour of cats, let's take a moment to talk more about them, how they interact with their environment, and how their brain processes. These are important to consider as they heavily influence many of the normal actions cats exhibit. A very important thing to keep in mind is: Cats don't feel or experience things the same way we do. As we discovered in the last chapter, they understand emotions differently. It's not surprising then that they perceive the world in another manner entirely. If you always anticipate your cat reacting a certain way (due to human-based expectations) you'll be disappointed when they never respond how you want. Taking a moment to acknowledge how cats typically react and perceive the world will allow for a better overall understanding of your companion. In time, leading to fewer hurt feelings and more realistic expectations for yourself.

How Cats Perceive the World

Much like us humans, cats rely heavily on their five senses to navigate the world around them. But there is quite a major contrast between us. Not only do their senses function differently than ours, but they are significantly sharper. Due to being hunters by nature, this design helps them find and track prey. But they also play a significant role in how your cat understands things in their environment (including you, your home, and just about anything they may come across). So, let's dive into discussing a bit more about our feline's astute senses.

While cats can have excellent eyesight, there are also quite a few drawbacks to how their eyes function, causing this to be one of their weaker senses. Cats are incapable of seeing some colours such as green and red: thus can't differentiate them from one another. On the other hand, they can see ultraviolet light, which gives them the ability to notice things that humans cannot. They have excellent depth perception, and their eyesight is focused more on movement. Both of these aid cats in hunting and allow them to notice and track smaller prey. They also don't have to blink to protect their eyes from drying out, thus enabling them to remain open and focused for as long as needed. Cats are, surprisingly, what is called middle-sighted. As the name suggests, this means cats have a hard time seeing things too far away, but also struggle with the opposite. To gain awareness of objects and animals in their spaces, they tend to rely on their other senses to make up for their eyes. A cat's optic layers can reflect light while the pupil dilates and constricts in specific lighting. The dilation allows them to see much better in low-light environments, thus benefiting their nightly hunting hours. However, while the pupils' constriction permits comfortable vision in brighter light, cats can't see quite as well in those environments. This daytime vision deficiency is made-up for by their ears.

One of their fairly strong senses is hearing—They can pick up an impressively wide range of sounds. This includes the low notes that humans can catch and also many higher-pitched sounds. Cats are even capable of sensing higher frequencies than a dog! They can detect various pitches and tones as well. This allows them to determine the almost exact location of noises up to three feet away, which plays a vital role in hunting down prey. They also perceive sounds coming from a massive distance and even hear four or five times farther than humans can! Cats move their ears independently from one another and can rotate them 180 degrees. These abilities allow them to track, detect, and pinpoint numerous vibrations.

In addition, touch is one of their more keen senses. While they do use their paws, bodies, or tails for various purposes (such as marking territory), the remarkable aspect of this sense is their whiskers. A cat's whiskers are incredibly sensitive, as its follicles are full of nerves and blood vessels. They are fairly similar to our fingertips. Aside from being cute, these hairs are vital to how your cat sees the world. They help with their vision by assisting in navigating their territory and the overall environment.

Whiskers don't feel anything but instead are used to transmit information. Whenever they touch other objects or sense movement in the air, a signal gets sent to bundles of nerves and various sensory cells. This whole process helps them to determine the shape, size, or speed of objects around them. With this ability, cats navigate the terrain expertly, even if they can't see that well. This also benefits cats in the wild, as whiskers help locate and track prey, plus detect potential enemies or predators. In addition, these hairs can help them stay balanced and aid cats to always land on their feet. Thanks to proprioceptors—located at the ends of whiskers—cats can detect what each part of their body is doing as well. The detection ability of whiskers aids cats in sensing the approach of small spaces; This tells them whether or not they can fit in the spot without getting stuck. Their whiskers can even protect their eyes from particles or objects that could potentially cause harm!

In contrast, a cat's sense of taste is another of its weaker ones. They tend to prefer fats and proteins, which is not too surprising since they are carnivores. However, they can't detect some flavors: such as sweet, fruity, or salty ones. They can also be avoidant of more bitter-tasting things. One of the most beneficial aspects of their taste aversion actually lies within their physical wellbeing. This taste aversion is because some of the flavors they typically dislike are potentially toxic to them. It also directly correlates with their sense of smell.

Notably, a cat's sense of smell is arguably its sharpest and most vital. Not only is it able to detect a shockingly wide array of things, but smells play a key part in terms of avoidance and other behaviours. Due to the importance of this sense, we'll go over it more in-depth in another chapter.

Emotions and Companionship

It's easy to believe that cats are not emotional animals, especially if you haven't had much personal experience with them. They seem to be more solitary and don't express emotions like we've come to expect from our pets. But just because they don't show it as openly as other pets or humans do, doesn't mean they don't feel strong emotions. Cats in the wild tend to hunt and live most of their lives alone. So they have evolved to express anger and aggression more aptly to protect themselves (and drive away predators or potential competition). Because they are far less domesticated and selectively bred than dogs, they are more connected with their baser instincts. To know how your cat feels, you must pay closer attention: Small, sometimes overlooked, gestures have importance.

Cats are a species that live their entire lives in the present. They don't think back on the past, nor do they plan for the future. They live here and now, so they base their decisions and emotions on what they are currently experiencing. Many of your cat's decisions are rooted in how they are feeling emotionally, especially those surrounding negative emotions. Because of this, they become easily influenced by their feelings and the current situation. They don't think through actions nor consider potential consequences; cats don't feel the more complex emotions that we do. This means if they are scared by something you did, they may lash out or hide without pondering over whether or not you even meant to scare them. All they know is that they are scared, and they need to react.

Your cat can feel a wide range of both positive and negative emotions, which you can often see expressed through different body language and changes in their general behaviour. They can be happy and content when in a safe environment, often leading to them feeling comfortable enough to rest, purr, or even knead. Or, they may become anxious when changes take place in the home. This can cause skittishness, hiding, or even confrontational and aggressive behaviour. The best way for you to understand your cat's emotions and feelings is to understand them from their point of view. Rather than expecting human-like emotions from them while showering them with love and affection, step back and allow your cat to initiate more. Over time, you'll come to notice and understand their behaviour with ease: Gaining the ability to tell what mood they are in with a glance.

When it comes to the natural order of things, cats don't necessarily need companions of any kind. In the wild, they are solitary hunters and spend most of their lives living alone. The only exceptions are when a female cat raises kittens or when a cat decides to live within a colony. But when it comes to completely domestic ones, who rely more on their human companions for food and affection, things are a bit different. It may not be a necessity for survival but, conversely, there is significant evidence that reveals cats enjoy the companionship of humans. Whether we notice it or not: They show they love us in all kinds of different and cat-like ways.

There are many different ways that cats show their love and affection toward their human companions, some of which may go unnoticed or get lost in your cat's normal behaviour. But if you know what to look for, you will be able to zero in on exactly when they are happy and comfortable. Purring and kneading are some of the most common—and obvious—signs of contentment, especially if they are resting near you or in your lap while doing so. When cats headbutt you or rub themselves against you, this is a sign of greeting while they simultaneously rub their smell all over you. Don't worry, that's a good sign! It's their way of essentially claiming you as theirs. Cats who meow at you are actually doing their best to communicate and connect with you, as adult felines typically don't meow at one another to communicate. This behaviour tends to be exclusively for their human companions. Cats who play with you or sleep around you are essentially including you in their typical routine. Not only do they find enjoyment in being around you, but they feel at ease in your presence. Also, if you find them grooming you, they see you as a fellow companion; This is a common social behaviour that is typically practiced and shared among cats.

Despite this, it may feel a bit disheartening when your cat doesn't shower you with the affection you expect from them (especially if you're accustomed to being around dogs). But just because they don't show it as clearly or readily as dogs do, doesn't mean your cat doesn't love you! Due to their base instincts, cats never really had a reason to worry about the feelings and affections of other animals around them. Their focus in the wild is surviving and ensuring that they find food and shelter, not the feelings of others. To put it simply, love and companionship—wild cats didn't need so much.

But quality time around your cat can easily change this for both you and your kitty. Research has shown that, over time, they will start to associate our smiles with positive emotions. In a study done at Oakland University, they found that cats who saw their owners smile reacted with positive behaviours, like purring or sitting in the laps of their owners. They typically did not react this way when their owner was frowning. Similarly, cats did not display the same behaviour when around strangers who were smiling or frowning. Researchers concluded: Cats learned over time alongside their owners that their smile was often associated with good things, such as playtime, food, getting pets, treats, and so on.

Research has also shown that cats can form strong attachments to their owners. They can display two types:

secure and insecure attachment. A cat possessing the first type: trusts its owner will take care of them, is willing to explore the surrounding area in a more relaxed manner, and sometimes will even investigate regions they are unfamiliar with as well. In a study done by Current Biology, cats who displayed this behaviour often greeted their owners when they entered the room but then returned to what they were originally doing. On the other hand, those with insecure attachments often displayed nervous or anxious behaviour with their owners. They would pace, twitch their tails, or even avoid their human companions when they returned to the room. This study found that about 64% of cats displayed secure attachment with their owners, which was a rather similar number when compared to dogs and human babies (Jackson, 2019). This study—and many other studies—on cats help to better understand their behaviour and show that they are more complex and dependent than some people may assume.

Routine and Safety

Interestingly enough, cats are actually very habitual creatures. They will fall into a groove and ensure they stick with it. In the wild, the best times for a cat to hunt and lay low, to avoid predators, dictate this routine. But when it comes to cats living with humans, their system is built around your habits. Being able to follow the schedule they have set makes them feel safe and comfortable. If something comes in abruptly and throws this off, your cat can experience severe stress and anxiety. If significant enough, it can cause even the healthiest cats to become ill and can have a long-lasting impact on your furry companion's health. Your cat relies on you as a source of comfort and stability, so you should do whatever you can to keep your kitty on their routine as much as possible. Doing so will keep your cat much happier and healthier. If you must change your shared routine, try to introduce the changes gradually to prevent a more stressful situation. Even minor changes can cause cats stress, so keep that in mind if you plan on altering your routine or daily life. This is especially necessary if you plan on making a significant change to your cat's environment.

If felines are not given a stable routine and environment, they can exhibit several negative and potentially harmful behaviours. Cats subjected to irregular patterns with their food, playtime, and socialization were more likely to hide, less likely to explore and relax in their environments, and were far more likely to urinate outside of their litter box. The concerning thing about this is a lot of domestic cats live in environments where their routines are often sporadic and unstable. While you may have your own schedule, likely, it's not nearly as strict as your cat's. Some days you may stay at work later, or maybe you decide to go out with your friends one weekend. Or you get sick, so you spend a few days at home. All of these things can throw your cat for a loop. Naturally, avoiding some of them isn't exactly easy, but there are ways you can try to keep your cat on their routine despite how much yours may change. Even when your schedule is haphazard, guarantee you can keep feeding and playtime on a strict timetable. This will give your cat an overall positive sense of stability and reassurance. Feeding times seem to be the most important in this aspect, and irregular feeding can cause a significant amount of stress for your cat. Make sure to have set meal times you follow daily, no matter what.

Perches and Caves

Cats have a habit of finding their way to the highest surface in the house. This could be your shelves, countertops, or even the top of fridges and cabinets. As with many of their more common habits, this is, once again, caused by their innate nature. In the wild, cats will perch from a high vantage point such as a tree or cliff. This view serves them several purposes. First, having this vantage point allows them to survey their territory, which enables them to spot predators or threats from a greater distance. They then have plenty of time to react to avoid conflict. Secondly, they can catch sight of prey, giving them an advantage to hunting down a nice meal.

So, while your pet may not need to survey their territory for threats or food, they still feel the need to climb up high. This need serves a different purpose for our more domesticated feline friends. But what is it?

For a house cat, having a perch allows them a space where they can feel safe and away from activity. It also enables kitties to be close to their owners simultaneously. These are great spots for your cat to escape stressful environments or to explore different areas of the home. Your cat could also perch on or around the window, which allows them to look out and watch things outside. Birds, squirrels, bugs, and even people passing can all provide them with entertainment.

Even if you live in a smaller space, you can use your cat's desire to climb to your advantage. Installing various ledges can allow them to climb, perch, and survey around your home. They should be at varying heights and placed in different locations around the more communal areas of the home. These can include cat trees, ledges on the walls, and those installed on and around windows. A good way to encourage them to sit by the window is to find ways to attract entertaining things into their view. Using feeders, for example, can help attract small critters closer to your window. Setting these up will not only make your cat feel safer and more comfortable, but it will also keep them entertained and encourage them to exercise.

It's incredible to watch your cat easily scale these vertically staggered ledges, and even more so when they decide to leap such a great height. They make it look so graceful and effortless, managing to almost always land on all fours! While the saying, "cats always land on their feet" isn't necessarily true, they can do so successfully a majority of the time. This ability coincides with their love of perching. Due to frequent climbing, their bodies have developed a process that helps to lessen potential damage from falls. It is called the "righting reflex".

Cats have something inside their ears known as the vestibular apparatus, which helps with orientation and balance. When falling, it helps them figure out which direction is up and enables them to turn their bodies the right way. They also lack a collarbone and have a flexible spine, both of which allow the complete turning of their torsos within a short amount of time. Their tail is actually an extension of their spine, meaning it plays a vital part in this process. The rotation of both their body and their tail together helps them to right themselves before they land on the ground.

Their legs are also built to help their bodies withstand the impact of falls. They're more muscular than they appear and absorb the shock of the collision. Their angled legs also assist in reducing this damage. On top of that, they are also able to slow their descent by spreading themselves out in a similar manner that flying squirrels do. This is due to the low volume-to-weight ratio in their bodies.

All of these abilities combined have allowed cats to leap, and fall, from incredible heights without much consequence. The likelihood of cats successfully landing on their feet—and walking away uninjured—depends a lot on the distance of the jump. Typically, the higher they're leaping from, the more likely they are to land safely. This is due to the time passing during the fall. The greater the height, the more time they have to rotate their bodies and adjust for impact, allowing them the chance to protect themselves. This ability is one of, if not the most, fascinating aspects of a cat.

On the other hand, cats tend to like the opposite of ledges: caves! Even if there are no natural caverns in your home for them to hide within, you may still find them squeezed into tight and confined spaces. Some of them may have you questioning: How in the world did they fit in there? Whenever they are sleeping, they are vulnerable and unprotected; Wild cats will often find enclosed spaces to rest to help ensure their safety. On top of that, they tend to curl themselves up into balls while sleeping. They have to protect those vital organs! These confined spaces will also provide them with warmth: Tucking themselves into this spot helps maintain their normal body temperature. Once again, this habit translates a little bit differently for indoor domestic cats. Rather than avoiding predators, they may seek these spaces to avoid noisy or annoying disruptions. That could be a dog or even a young child who feels like a threat to their peaceful rest. Cats prefer to avoid conflict whenever they can. So they would rather flee to their confined spots to hide until the stressor is gone.

To keep your home comfortable for your kitty, you should provide plenty of spaces to conceal themselves within. You can find all sorts of cat caves in the store. There are also cat trees that come with built-in cave portions connected. Crates and boxes with soft blankets inside also work for pleasant kitty burrows. Having a variety of these throughout the house will ensure they feel safe, even in the face of potential stressors of all sorts. It would be a good idea to have a few caves set up within the communal places in your house as well. That will enable your cat to stick close to you if they want. If you find that your cat is hiding where you don't want them to: such as under your bed, in the closet, or in other potentially unsafe places— There are a few ways to alter this. One such way is to entice them to the safer burrowing spots by putting something that smells like you, such as a shirt or a blanket, in those places. Your scent will attract and comfort your cat, making them feel more inclined to hide away in these places.

Even if you give your cat some more roomy caves to choose from, you may find them squeezed into odd spaces. Some of the biggest cats can manage to squish themselves into impossibly small things. Much like their impressive climbing and jumping abilities, it has a lot to do with their flexibility. Since they don't have a collarbone, they have a much easier time fitting their heads and shoulders into a small space. After that, it's easy for the rest of their body to follow. Typically cats are very lean, allowing them to fit just about anywhere. Be sure to keep an eye out in case of possible dangerous situations where they could become injured or stuck. No one wants a hurt kitty cat!

Chapter 3: Typical Feline Behaviour

Cats can be difficult to read if you don't exactly know what you're looking for. Nevertheless, becoming more conscious of their common quirks will give you the ability to realize what your cat is feeling and thinking. That will not only make life easier for you and your companion, but it will also clue you in on when your cat's typical moods shift, which can signal that something is wrong.

Being able to read your cat's mood has a lot to do with picking up on their usual vocalizations and body language. While they aren't the most expressive, and sometimes not all that vocal, they do have plenty of indications toward their mood that you can learn to read. Aside from these things, there are a lot of typical mannerisms you should keep an eye out for as well. Having a cat who actively pounces and plays is a sign they are energized and happy. While normal grooming is indicative of their wellbeing. The list goes on!

Their more positive behaviours can express various levels of happiness; The negative ones can tell you when your cat is feeling upset or when they may be physically or emotionally unwell. If you notice your cat is displaying unfavorable mannerisms, you must assess the situation to figure out the cause. Your cat could be trying to express that they're feeling anxious or stressed. On the other hand, they could be showing you that they are injured, sick, or potentially developing a serious health condition. Should they start displaying these kinds of behaviours, especially abruptly, you may need to take a trip to the vet. Remember that your cat can't tell you directly when something is wrong, so it's up to their human companions to notice when their habits change.

Body Language

Body language is considered a universal language among humans, but the same could be said for cats. Being able to read and comprehend the mannerisms of your feline companion is a vital part of noticing the mood they are in and the emotions they are experiencing. While their vocalizations can tell you what they are feeling, the capacity to understand their gestures reveals emotions in a way that their voice can't do alone.

When using a cat's body language to determine their mood, you should make sure to take in their overall stature rather than focusing on a few specific indicators. Typically the different positions of the expressive parts of your cat all work together to indicate varied emotions. Taking a step back to assess will give you a better perception of their overall mood. We will be breaking down and discussing the specific parts of a cat's body language. Though, it's important to remember that expressions can mean different things depending on context and vary between cats. As long as you understand the basics and know your cat well, you can successfully determine their mood through non-verbal cues.

The context and overall setting are other major factors in this. Try to understand the situation from the perspective of your cat rather than your own. Even if you have the best intentions, approaching a cowering feline, who is avoiding your touch, can end badly for both of you. You should take into account the environment they are in and the people and animals around them. If they are in a confined space and surrounded by strangers, they are far less likely to be receptive toward your advances. However, if they are in a more open area with you or other people they trust, they are more likely to allow you to approach. Also, take note of the different sounds, sights, and smells that could affect your cat's mood. Looking at the 'big picture' before trying to determine how they are feeling can help you decide how to approach them and how they could potentially react.

The mannerisms of a happy and confident cat are ones that you should see throughout their more active periods. They will typically have their ears up and facing forward: which indicates various positive emotions, such as happiness, confidence, or calmness. Alternatively, if their ears are high and they continue to swivel or twitch, they are more excited and alert. They may be ready to play or in an overall rambunctious mood. You can also look into their eyes, or more specifically, their pupils. If their pupils are relaxed, then this could indicate your cat is also relaxed. On the other hand, a playful kitty will have wide, dilated ones; They are probably ready to pounce on their toy! You may notice that when your cat is happy or content, they will blink slowly at you. It is a well-known sign of affection and trust. If you ever notice them doing it, maybe try slow blinking back at them to return the gesture. Their whiskers can also be very telling, as a joyful cat will keep them forward. An alert and happy feline will also have its tail raised straight in the air. That can also express confidence or overall comfort in their environment. They may quiver their tail when they are particularly excited, which they often exhibit when greeting you once you have arrived home.

Furthermore, cats tend to point their bodies in the direction that they plan to go. If they have a relaxed posture and are turned directly toward you, then they are receptive and comfortable with you. They may also be conveying a desire to interact with you; They could be looking for affection or a play session. However, this doesn't necessarily mean that a cat with its back to you is uninterested in you! Doing so has put them at a disadvantage, as they have let their guard down—It's possible they feel extra comfortable around you. Make sure to remember to look for other context clues to be certain. Cats who stretch themselves out whenever they're near you are often exposing very vulnerable parts of their body in the process. These mannerisms are typically very positive and are another way to show the level of comfort they feel in your presence. If you go to pet your cat and they arch themselves up to meet your hand, they are very happy with the attention you are giving them. This could be paired with them purring and rubbing against your legs.

Alternatively, cats who are frightened or nervous will often use various ways to make themselves appear smaller. This is to try and go undetected or unbothered but also to protect themselves from potential attacks. They will lower themselves to the floor and keep their tails low, or even tucked beneath them. This position makes them appear more compact and provides the ability to spring away and flee with ease. Cats will also flatten their ears sideways (affectionately referred to as 'airplane ears') and pull their whiskers closer to their face. They often have wide pupils in these instances, with very focused attention. If they were only briefly spooked, they may simply react with bristled fur. Raised hackles or a bushy tail could be the response to loud noise or a startling movement.

Angry and confrontational cats, on the other hand, do the exact opposite. They try to make themselves appear bigger and more intimidating to scare the source of their anger away. They will stand sideways and arch their backs as high as possible while simultaneously bristling their fur out, raising their bushy tail. Doing this shows that they are ready to fight if it comes to that. Ears folded back and constricted pupils convey hostility. They will also push their whiskers forward to add to their threatening appearance. This level of anger doesn't appear abruptly, however, and there are a few more subtle signs that may indicate your cat is becoming frustrated. If you notice your cat flicking its tail back and forth, they are likely trying to express their annoyance. The faster that their tail is going, the angrier they are getting—A sure sign to back off!

Belly Exposure

The most sensitive and vulnerable area of a cat's body is their belly. Many people have probably heard that if they show you their stomach, it means that they feel comfortable, safe, and relaxed around you. While this may be true for many cats and could even be the case for yours, it is not always the case. This pose could also mean that they are ready to strike at a moment's notice as this position is the easiest way for them to defend themselves with their claws.

The best way to tell which mood your kitty is in is by looking at their other non-verbal cues. If their tail is still, their eyes are closed or unfocused, and they generally seem relaxed, then they are likely resting on their back. However, if their tail is twitching and they seem more alert and focused, then they are ready to pounce the moment your hand gets too close. Ensuring that you gauge their overall disposition before deciding to pet them will help keep you from falling victim to their claws.

Kneading

When cats are flexing their paws against material in a rhythmic manner, they are kneading against something. Typically this action is paired with a content, purring kitty. This behaviour stems from early kittenhood. Kittens knead against their mother's belly to stimulate the production of milk when they want to nurse. But even much older adult cats still carry this behaviour. They will knead beds, blankets, toys, or anything soft they can get their paws on. They may even knead you, often when they are happily resting in your lap. It is their way of showing they love you and how happy they are to be with you. While often taken as a sign of affection, there are some other reasons that cats will often knead.

Aside from just showing happiness and contentment, cats also knead for comfort. Practicing this behaviour against soft and plush objects will remind them of the warmth and comfort of kittenhood. To express their happiness, they will often purr on top of it. When they do this, they are typically very relaxed and happy—You should take this as a great sign. Your kitty feels safe and comfortable in your home! Kneading can help cats to stretch out their various muscles, keeping them limber and flexible. They may decide to knead things to mark their belongings and owners as their possessions. Cats have scent glands in their paws; Kneading helps spread their scent against the objects they view as their territory. You should take their need to mark you with their scent as a good thing! They see you as part of their family and want to make sure other cats don't try to claim you.

Loafing

You may notice at times while your cat is resting that they've chosen to settle in a loafing position. Affectionately called this because they look like a loaf of bread, they seem both comfortable and adorable while doing this.

But why do they pick such a unique position to lay in? For one thing, it's relaxing and comfortable. They're so content within their environment that they've chosen to hide their paws. This is a sign that they don't feel any level of threat or danger. They could also be doing it for a more practical reason. Laying in this position helps them to conserve body heat. They could be feeling a little chilly and decided to loaf to warm themselves back up. No matter the reason, if you find your kitty resting in this position, know that they are one warm and happy loaf.

Scratching and Biting

There are many reasons a cat may be biting or scratching at you or on surfaces in your home. It is one of the few ways they can communicate with us, so try to pay attention to the reason behind the action rather than getting frustrated immediately. They may bite because they've been startled by something or perhaps because they're angry and stressed.

A cat may bite because they are getting too much affection when they would prefer to be left alone. It's important to watch their behaviour in these instances, which can help you avoid getting bitten in the first place. If they start to show some of those frustrated or annoyed body language cues, stop and give them some space. They may even give a few gentle warning bites or open their mouths as though they want to bite. It's up to you to pick up on these so that your cat doesn't have to resort to biting you. Give them space and let them approach you for affection instead.

As far as scratching goes, cats will often scratch on different surfaces to mark their territory. As mentioned before, they have scent glands within their paws. Not only does the scratching cause a noticeable mark, but it also leaves their scent. They may even do this on purpose in front of another animal to declare the object as theirs. Because of this, they often target important and communal places, such as near the food, near litter boxes, or around resting areas.

During playtime, or even when doing simple tasks such as jumping on your lap, cats may accidentally end up scratching you in the process. You mustn't react with anger or aggression, even if it does hurt. If it was accidental, they likely didn't realize that they did it, and they certainly don't know that it hurt you. Lashing out will only confuse them and potentially stress them out.

If your cat is scratching, biting, or chewing on themselves excessively, there could be something medically wrong. This behaviour can lead to fur loss, as well as skin damage. If they are missing patches of fur or have irritated skin, they are likely biting or scratching themselves excessively. The first thing to rule out is parasites, especially fleas, which can cause this behaviour due to the irritation they create. They may be difficult to notice at first. Cats are very meticulous at grooming and tend to hide that they have fleas. Searching for them or potential scratches left behind caused by the itchiness may yield some results. You may also notice these parasites biting you as well! Should the mannerisms not be caused by fleas, the behaviour may be due to a health problem. Your cat could have an allergy to something in their environment or even their food, or they could have developed dry skin. If they are targeting a specific area, then they could be feeling pain from that spot. This is one of those red flag behaviours we mentioned earlier in this chapter, so ensure that you thoroughly investigate any potential external or physical cause. Once you have eliminated these possibilities, you will be left with the final possible trigger: boredom! Your pet's environment needs to be stimulating to ensure that they never have to resort to excessive biting for entertainment.

Playing

Playing is typical behaviour among cats. Not only is it natural, it is also beneficial to them in several ways. Playing with toys encourages them to act on their instincts to hunt, stalk, and pounce. That will help them let out a lot of their energy and keep them active despite being unable to hunt in the wild. If you have multiple cats, they will often play with one another, which helps them form their social bonds. Alternatively, when you actively play with your kitty, you are helping to strengthen the bond that you share with them.

There are typically two different kinds of play that a cat will partake in: solitary play and social play. As expected, solitary play is when they play alone. Typically this means they are playing with various toys or other objects they can get their claws on. Cats have even been known to play with boxes, paper, hair ties, and other random things they may find around the house. Social play is when they play with another animal. While this is typically another cat, it can also describe the play sessions you have with them, or even when they play with other animals such as dogs.

The key part to telling the difference between harmless play and aggression is the body language and behaviour of the pair. Two cats who are facing off aggressively will be hard to miss. They will show clear signs of aggression, or one may show signs of stress and discomfort, and they will likely emit a range of loud and angry noises. If this behaviour repeats often, something may need to change to establish a safe home and environment for both cats. Those who are just partaking in typical social play are easy to pick up on as well. They will stalk and pounce on one another, bite and scratch, and even chase each other around the house. But this behaviour is normal between cats. They learned this from a young age, and they often practiced this manner of play on their siblings or unsuspecting mother. Social play is a good practice for your cats; It helps them build social relationships and productively exert their energy. This play may appear rough and aggressive when you're watching it, but keep in mind that this is typical. So long as it doesn't escalate into aggression and neither of them show signs of genuine fear or hostility.

While this behaviour is completely normal for cats, it's not uncommon for them to direct their play toward their human companions. In theory, this isn't a bad thing, but they don't realize their typical play habits can be physically harmful to us. We don't have the fur to protect us against their claws and teeth, so their attempts often result in us getting injured—and boy, do cat scratches and bites hurt! They can also become easily infected due to bacteria on their claws. If your cat has started doing this, try not to react with aggression. After all, they're only trying to play with you. They don't realize the damage they could potentially be causing. Instead, try to redirect them toward a toy and engage with them in an active play session. Doing so teaches your kitty they are only allowed to target designated toys and helps them exert their energy.

Hunting

Cats are hunters by nature. You may often see these instincts come out when they play with other cats or chase after their toys. Due to the severe lack of selective breeding, even your house cat who never set a paw outside can be a successful hunter should they get the chance. Feeding your pet the normal and healthy amount can curb many of their desires to hunt. Yet it's still possible you may find them stalking and hunting any prey they may find; Especially if your cat is allowed outside.

So, if they aren't being motivated by hunger, why are they still hunting prey for themselves? Due to cats being solitary hunters, they can only rely on themselves for their food. As such, they have to hunt whenever they can to keep themselves fed. If they only did so when they were hungry, they would risk running out of energy and potentially being unable to hunt. Even if cats are excellent hunters, it is still a difficult task, and they are not always successful. Ultimately, they would starve if they didn't ensure they had backup food. Due to this they are opportunistic hunters. Being in their nature, if they get the opportunity to hunt down a tasty meal, they will take it. This is also why the prey they hunt may be left uneaten. Alternatively, your cat may hunt to try out some new flavors. They like tasting varieties of food and could be looking for a different taste than their typical meal.

If you've ever watched your cat hunt, you may have seen them 'play' with whatever prey they were trying to catch. Many people see this as tormenting the animal they are hunting and may even see it as cruel behaviour. This is what is known as displacement behaviour. They are conflicted about hunting their prey: Torn between their need for food and their fear of potentially being harmed by the animal they are stalking. The more fearful they are, the more likely they are to play with the prey.

Pouncing

Much like hunting and stalking, pouncing is all instinct and ties in rather heavily with their predatory nature. You will often see your cat pouncing on things such as toys or other cats whenever they are engaging in play. Their pouncing shouldn't become an issue, so long as they are provided a fun, enriching environment alongside plenty of toys and play sessions. This is especially true if you are keeping them strictly indoors.

It is fun to watch your cat pouncing on toys, but when it turns on you, it can become frustrating and painful. Sometimes, they will hide behind things or around corners, preparing to jump on you and attack your toes and feet. While they may see this as playing and are exhibiting the normal pouncing and playing mannerisms, it can be startling. It could also result in injury if they aren't redirected from using you as a toy. Oftentimes, they do this to get your attention and tell you that they want to play. The best way to avoid this is by surrounding your pet in an environment full of claw-safe toys they can use instead. You also want to ensure to dedicate time throughout your day to play with your cat. Things such as laser pointers or cat toy wands could work for this specific habit. These toys allow your cat to chase, pounce, and hunt something that isn't you.

While this is the most common reason, cats may also be pouncing on you due to external stressors or medical reasons. They could be trying to communicate with you, or they may have chosen you as their target to take out their frustrations. This is another one of those mannerisms that require investigation if it comes on abruptly. It was likely triggered by something specific.

Grooming

Cats are fairly meticulous groomers and often spend a large amount of their time awake cleaning themselves. This behaviour is learned from kittenhood and serves several different purposes. Not only does it benefit their health, but it can function as a social behaviour and help them bond with other animals, which includes you.

One of the biggest reasons cats groom themselves so frequently is for health and wellness purposes. When they lick their fur, it helps to stimulate the production of sebum: An oil produced within the hair follicles. Spreading it across their fur helps to protect it and give it that shine; Keeping both their skin and fur healthy. Because cats do not sweat to cool themselves, they instead do so by grooming themselves. After licking their fur, the evaporation of the saliva helps to cool them down. The process also helps remove dirt and tangles from the cat's fur; It can even remove parasites such as fleas and ticks. Paying attention to their physical appearance can be a good indication of their health and wellbeing. If they are often ungroomed, it is possible that they aren't feeling well enough or they are physically unable to look after themselves.

Grooming can help a cat soothe themselves when they are emotionally strained. They may even default to grooming if they are unsure how to react to a situation. They tend to find comfort in the behaviour. While typically this isn't a problem, if you find your cat grooming themselves excessively and giving themselves bald patches or damaging their skin, they could be very distressed. This is another potential red flag behaviour that should be investigated, similarly to the excessive biting and scratching.

If you own multiple cats, you will likely see them engaging in what is called mutual grooming. As implied by the name, this is when they bathe one another. It's a social activity that can help to build their relationship. It also helps in a general cleanliness way—Having someone else groom them helps reach the spots that are difficult to get to alone. Cats even mirror this behaviour to their human companions. As mentioned in previous chapters, this is one of the ways that they show affection.

Vocalizations

Some cats may not always be the most expressive verbally, especially when it comes to their more positive emotions. This can cause many owners to be unsure about what their pet is feeling. Truthfully the amount of meowing, purring, and chirping you hear from your cat is going to depend entirely on their personality. Each kitty is different in many ways, and that includes how much they are willing to chat. Even the pitch and volume of their meow is going to vary.

External factors can potentially influence just how vocal they are. For example, if a kitten is handled by and around humans more at a young age, they tend to grow into chatty adults. Also, as cats get older, they could become more vocal due to their deteriorating senses or their mental state becoming impaired because of age. Truthfully, the best way to know what your cat is trying to say is to just spend time with them. While we will go over the basics so that you have a general understanding of the common sounds, that won't account for the personal habits of your kitty—and that's okay! The more time you spend living alongside your furry companion, the better you'll be able to pick up on what they're trying to tell you. With that in mind, let's dive into the basics.

Meowing is one of the most common vocalizations you'll probably hear from them. All cats tend to meow as kittens, but wild adults hardly ever meow. On the other hand, those living with humans meow a significant amount. It is one of the ways that they try to communicate with us. Meowing can mean a wide range of things. They could be simpler reasons, such as wanting food, craving some of your attention, or maybe they're meowing just to meow. Alternatively, the meows could be for a more serious reason, such as stress, anxiety, or they could be trying to tell you they're hurt or not ill. Some of them are a lot more vocal than others are, so the amount of meowing, the sound, and the volume will differ from your cat and another. The best way to determine why they are meowing is to study their body language and the environmental factors. These can help clue you in on what may be causing your kitty to call for you. More time spent with them will allow you to learn your cat's different meows easier so that you can know what they want just from listening. If you notice they are meowing almost excessively, or seem to be doing so much more than usual, there could be something wrong. Once more, this is one of the behaviours you will need to investigate to find the potential cause or stressor.

Oftentimes, when your cat is purring, it's a rather good indication of their happiness. If your pet is nestled in your lap or curled up in their favorite spot and is constantly purring, then this is a sign that they are relaxed and content. However, there can be times when your cat may purr when they are stressed or anxious. It is essentially a method of calming themselves down or soothing themselves. It's important to pay attention to their body language in this situation. If they are displaying some of the nervous or stressed non-verbal cues that we covered earlier, despite purring, then a stressor likely caused the sound. If your cat is sick or injured, you may notice them purring to themselves as well. Not only is this a method of soothing, but it is believed that the sound could help stimulate the healing process. Some research even suggests that the low frequency of the sound could potentially go so far as to help repair bones, build muscle, and accelerate healing, among other things. There is speculation that this could be why cats seem to recover from falls and other injuries so much faster than dogs do.

Trills or chirps are another rather common sound you'll hear from your cat. They're more high-pitched than regular meowing and are typically made to get our attention for something. They learned this sound as kittens; Their mothers would use it to get their babies to focus on her. So, they now use it on you for the same reason. Maybe they see something that they want to show you, or they want to lead you somewhere; This sound is often your cat's way of saying 'Hey! Look at me! Follow me!' They may also trill to express how happy and excited they are. Rather than meowing, chirps and trills are the noise most cats use when communicating with one another. If you have more than one, you may notice them chirping at each other.

The chatter or chitter is something they may do whenever they're sitting by a window and spot a bird or a squirrel outside. It's an interesting little noise, and your cat makes quite the cute movement with their mouth in the process. This noise may also sound a bit more like a squeak. It essentially translates to excitement at seeing something that they could chase. It is also potentially linked to the frustration at not being able to get to that prey. The creature on the other side of the glass has triggered their desire and need to hunt. Yet, they are separated by the window, meaning your cat can't do anything about it. Thus the noise they emit is a mixture of those two feelings.

Additionally, if your cat feels threatened or scared, they tend to go through an entire series of hostile vocalizations.

These sounds increase in intensity the longer the threat is nearby, thus mirroring their rising hostility or fear. This series of sounds will often start with a growl. Typically low and threatening, this sound is a warning toward the threat. If a growling cat is ever making this noise at you, you should acknowledge that warning by backing off and giving them space. Typically, this vocalization is paired with the defensive body language we discussed, such as an arched back, bristled fur, and folded ears. As long as they are not in any danger, you should leave a cat who is growling alone and allow them to calm down. If you can determine what is causing the aggression, then try to remove it from the environment so it feels less threatened and begin to relax.

The next step in the sounds is a hiss. Another threat, this vocalization also allows your cat to show off those teeth as another warning. This sound may also be paired with spitting. Much like when your cat is growling, they will likely show angry and aggressive body language, including bared fangs, raised hackles, and a twitching tail. In this case, they may be ready to strike at whatever they perceive as a threat to them.

Once again, give cats using these vocalizations space to relax and try removing whatever they are threatened by from their environment. How often you hear these sounds from your pet can vary significantly between cats. Some are just naturally more relaxed and calm, while others are more easily startled or defensive. These traits can depend on personality, environment, or even where they came from and what they experienced. However, significant changes in their environment can potentially make even the calmest cat defensive and hostile. Make sure to keep an eye out for this and keep your pet's territory comfortable to help avoid any growling or hissing.

Hissing can escalate to a yowl or howl, their vocalizations rising in volume and aggression as they continue to feel threatened and uncomfortable. It is a fairly loud and drawn-out noise. If your cat does not feel hostile or threatened, then they may be distressed in some way. They could be stuck somewhere, are sick or in pain, have found some other animal they don't know in their territory, or they could even be looking for you and can't seem to find you. If your pet is making this noise, make sure to find them and try to determine what is wrong. This is also a noise that non-spayed females may make whenever they are in heat, as they are trying to get the attention of males with the noise.

If you have an older cat or one that is cognitively disabled, they may make this noise more often due to how disoriented they can become. If your cat is making this noise more frequently, you should check for signs of injury, illness, or other potential causes for concern. Make sure your cat has lots of toys to play with, gets attention from you, and feels comfortable and safe in their environment. After all, the noise could simply be from boredom.

The final sound they will make in this series of aggressive noises is a shriek. They are signaling that they are done threatening, and since the subject of their threats has not backed off, they will take the next step of the conflict. They are prepared to either run and avoid further confrontation or to take it head-on. They may follow the vocalizations with a pounce. If you have two shrieking cats, then it is likely that a fight is about to break loose if it hasn't already. Try to break up any conflict like this as safely as possible!

Chapter 4: The Importance of Smell

Out of all of their senses, cats rely the most on their sense of smell. Not only do they use it to discern where various territory markers are, but it's very helpful in tracking prey. Their impressively strong noses can also tell them a multitude of things about any of the other cats that they happen to meet. On top of that, they have even developed strong aversions to certain smells, which occasionally belong to things that could be toxic if ingested.

A feline's sense of smell is about 14 times stronger than ours, and can even rival the scenting abilities of some dog breeds. Cats have about 45 to 80 million scent receptors within their noses; Some even believe that they could potentially have up to 200 million. When compared to humans, who only have about 5 million, their sense of smell is exceedingly more sophisticated than ours. That's amazing, right?—*Wait for it*—Cats also have an additional organ that helps them to smell! Called the Jacobson's organ, or the vomeronasal organ, it is located inside of the roof of their mouths. Have you ever seen your cat pull its lips back or open its mouth whenever it smelled something? That's them using their Jacobson's organ! This organ serves as a secondary source of detection, but rather than picking up scents, it detects chemicals. This means that cats can detect substances that don't actually have a smell. Nerves within this organ lead directly to their brain, giving it fascinating capabilities.

Not only does this organ help cats be able to smell better, but it also helps them in a lot of practical ways. For one, the organ helps aid in reproduction, as it assists them in picking up on the different pheromones of cats in their area and whether or not they are available. They also use this sense of smell to detect cats within their territory. Specifically, it's used to recognise and determine if other felines are friendly or potential enemies. Besides that, this enhanced sense of smell helps kittens find their mother's milk. Newborns are known to have skillfully located their mother when set between multiple nursing dams.

Their sense of smell is also very important when it comes to interacting with other cats. When meeting, they use their nose and smell, rather than a handshake or a hug, to greet their fellow cats. When first interacting, they will sniff around each other's head areas, or may even bump them together in order to detect pheromones. Doing so will allow them to know more about one another through their scents. It may seem surprising or almost like a superpower, but through smell alone, a cat can tell what sex the other cat is, what kind of mood they are in, and even what their health is like. While this is possible through just sniffing one another's heads, it's much easier to get this information upon investigating a bit closer. This is why they often sniff each other's rear ends. Doing so gives them that information, and even more, such as telling them whether they've met the other cat before. This act can also show dominance between the two. The dominant one will typically initiate the interaction with the submissive cat following suit soon after.

The Jacobsen's organ also helps significantly when detecting the potential of a smell to lead them to toxic objects. Using their ability to detect the chemical aspects of different smells, they can sometimes determine when these scents are coming from possibly dangerous objects or plants. Over time, the ability to detect these components has caused many cats to dislike the smells of toxic and dangerous things. This has had a lot of evolutionary benefits for them as a whole. Despite the impressiveness of their noses, not every cat gets deterred by smells of toxic flowers and other objects! It's vitally important not to bring poisonous things into your home your cat may ingest.

While most of the smells that cats dislike seem to be rooted in toxicity, that isn't always the case. Some may even enjoy the scent of potentially dangerous things. But just like their tastes in food, cats have personal preferences when it comes to smells. Knowing what types your pet likes and dislikes can help you decide what fragrances to bring into the home So be sure to pick just the right ones to help keep both of you happy!

What Scents Cats Like

Catnip is one of the scents that tend to attract most cats. Catnip can stimulate their brain and put them in a playful and hyperactive mood. This can cause them to lick, rollover, eat, and pounce on whatever smells of catnip; It's inclined to have a rather strong effect on your cat. The scent and overall effects of catnip are typically rather popular among felines; It's been a reliable go-to when searching for inexpensive and exciting toys or treats for your companion. However, if you have a cat who doesn't seem to enjoy catnip as most kitties do, it may be a good idea to try valerian root instead. This plant has a fairly similar effect on them as catnip does; Although the biggest difference is it significantly relaxes cats once the hyperactive effects wear off. They will become drowsy and calm—a natural sedative of sorts that could help your cat before a stressful event, such as a car ride to the vet.

Similarly, olive can be as relaxing on cats as catnip. They tend to rub against it, eat it, or lick it; But rather than putting them in an excited and active mood: Olive has a more calming effect. Exposure to this plant may even put your cat in a laid-back disposition, thus helping to calm more nervous kitties. While some cats are more attracted to the leaves, others are attracted to the actual olives or olive-containing products.

In addition, honeysuckle can also be relieving for cats and be used to help soothe those dealing with anxiety or stress. While they are drawn to the fragrance and want to lick and bite it, ingesting honeysuckle (especially the berries) can be dangerous to cats. Due to this, they should only be allowed to enjoy the fragrance of it.

Thyme is a fragrance that may only attract some cats, while others may not be nearly as interested in it. Even so, thyme can be rather beneficial for your kitty. The scent of it is relaxing to them and, like honeysuckle, can help calm those with anxiety. On top of that benefit, thyme works as an excellent anti-inflammatory for your cat. Thus, the plant can help those who suffer from allergies or other irritations.

Similar to thyme, chamomile may attract some cats, while others may show little interest. Another calming herb that can help with allergies or inflammation: A good alternative when your kitty seems uninterested in thyme. Also rather relaxing, it can be toxic if consumed in large amounts; For this reason, it's a good idea to expose your pet to minimal amounts.

Overall, there are quite a few floral scents that cats seem to appreciate, and the specifics of what kinds of flowers are enjoyed will differ between cats. However, many flowers are toxic to cats, one of the most dangerous being lilies. Whenever bringing flowers into your home, or allowing your cat near them, make sure to check that they are safe to be around your pet.

Another general group of smells cats enjoy is fruits. While there are some specific fruits they dislike, they seem to enjoy the scent of a few others, such as watermelon and strawberry. In fact, if you find that your kitty enjoys the smell of some fruit, they may even enjoy the taste of them. Snacking on cat-safe fruits could give your pet various benefits, such as vitamins and antioxidants. Always make sure to cut them into small pieces before trying and check the safety of anything fed to your pet. Fruits such as apples, pineapples, and blueberries can be a nice, healthy occasional snack for your furry companion.

Next, mint is one of those scents that some cats love and some hate. Those that love it are typically drawn to it due to its relation to catnip, despite mint itself being toxic to cats. There are several scents related to it that fall in the same category. Peppermint, for example, may attract some cats and deter others, despite its toxicity. Spearmint and other similar mints may also attract them; Though these are far less toxic than peppermint is. If your kitty is attracted to certain mint-related scents, make sure to be conscious of what kind and do some research on its toxicity.

Lastly, basil is another herbal scent that some cats may enjoy. It is within the same family as catnip, which is likely why this occurs, as it can have somewhat of a similar effect on them. However, they aren't quite so keen on eating basil. Cats don't enjoy the flavor, despite it being non-toxic to them. Keeping some around for the smell may be a good idea, especially if your cat seems to enjoy it.

What Scents Cats Dislike

Cats hate the strong smell of all kinds of citrus and are typically even deterred from trying to taste them. In fact, many people who garden use citrus peels to deter strays from them. While they can safely eat citrus, the peels and plant portions can make them sick.

Hot peppers are another strong scent that cats dislike. Many strong spicy smells tend to deter them, including cinnamon and curry. They may perceive these smells as toxic. While cinnamon is safe for them to consume, you should avoid letting your cat ingest any sort of peppers or pepper flakes as they can make them sick.

Besides citrus, there are quite a few herbs that could potentially deter your feline. Although this isn't guaranteed, as some cats dislike certain scents more than others do. Herbs such as lavender, rosemary, marigolds, rue, geranium, and eucalyptus can cause them to turn up their noses. The biggest reason for this is that many of these plants are toxic to cats if they ingest them. Given that, they have developed a strong dislike for many different plants and herbs as a sort of defense mechanism.

Surprisingly, the scent of bananas is a specific smell that cats don't like, even though ingesting it won't cause any harm to them. Due to how strong the smell of pine is, cats tend to be put off by it as well. Try to avoid things, such as litter, heavily scented with pine as it could keep your kitty from using the litter box or interacting with the item.

Next, vinegar is a common cat deterrent, and non-toxic to them. It can be used for cleaning or to deter cats from places and objects. Some strong chemical smells will not only bother your cat's sensitive nose but can also be toxic. When choosing your cleaning products, especially those used to clean objects pets interact with, make sure to utilize more natural cleaners and ones that aren't so strongly scented.

As mentioned before, some mint-related smells may attract, while others deter cats. This can vary between them, but some mint smells most cats greatly dislike. Wintergreen, for example, not only tends to deter most but is highly toxic to them. Menthol is another strong, minty scent that cats prefer to avoid.

Of course, the smell of a dirty litter box is a huge deterrent for cats. This is especially true if you have a multi-cat household. If their litter box is too full they may be compelled to find somewhere else to use the bathroom. Ensure you have enough litter boxes for your cats and that you clean them regularly so this doesn't happen.

Finally, essential oils are a huge deterrent for cats. Due to how sensitive their senses are, the intense and compounded smell of the oils can be overwhelming to them. That aside, a lot of them are very toxic to cats. They can't break down some toxins due to a lack of the enzyme needed in their liver. As such, things such as the phenols in essential oils can poison cats. Whether the particles are airborne and inhaled or are ingested after being groomed off of their fur, they can cause serious health issues for our pets. Even worse is if they manage to ingest the liquid directly, which could potentially lead to liver failure and death. There is a range of essential oils that you should absolutely avoid using if you have a cat.

While these dangers don't necessarily mean you shouldn't use them at all, it does mean you should be careful and use them in serious moderation. Make sure to research the specific essential oil you are looking to use to ensure it's safe to be around your cats. Always check the labels of the brands you're purchasing to avoid accidentally getting ones containing phenols.

Keep the oils in a safe place that they can't access, and always keep an eye on any diffuser you may be using.

In general, make sure to double-check everything for the safety of your cat. If they become ill and you suspect they may have come into contact with essential oils, take them to the vet immediately.

Chapter 5: Cats and Their Territory

As we have discussed before, cats are still very in touch with their more wild and natural instincts. In the wild, being territorial is necessary for them to survive and thrive in their environment. Especially if resources are more limited in that area. But how does this translate to your little house cat? Well, our cats see their environments, and thus our homes, as their territory. Because of this, they tend to mark various things within as parts of their 'territory'. This could include beds, toys, or even you.

Cats have scent glands in various parts of their bodies, including their toes, lips, cheeks, head, and tail. So, a lot of behaviours you may notice from your feline could also be them marking something as theirs. For instance, as mentioned before, when your cat scratches on a surface, they are leaving their scent on it and claiming it. They will also practice bunting against objects in the home, in which they rub their cheeks and face against things. This process puts their scent all over the object. This is why you often see them rubbing their faces on toys or the corners of the couch and your bed.

Another common way that cats mark territory, especially non-neutered males, is through urine. The smell of this is incredibly strong and is used to mark their region, to keep other males out of the claimed space. The best way to avoid a male cat behaving in this manner, especially if they are exclusively indoors, is to get him neutered. However, if you find your fixed cats of either sex are urinating outside of their litterbox, there may be another cause. Some cats will resort to this behaviour whenever stressed or anxious: Being around their own familiar scent brings them a level of comfort.

Cats who live in the wild, or are considered strays, often have a rather large domain that they stake their claim over. Not to mention, they tend to establish their own schedules for themselves: dedicating spaces and times for hunting, eating, and sleeping.

Usually, they prefer to be solitary animals, and rather than fighting for land or developing behaviours to determine who will stake their claim over resources, they have formed ways to secure their territory. Scent marking, which includes scratching on trees (or objects) and urinating in different places, keeps strays away from their lands. But they also participate in defensive and aggressive behaviours by using their angry body language and vocalizations to scare other cats away. Cats try to avoid conflict as much as possible, so they prefer to rely on this tactic as a prevention method whenever possible.

Territory is vitally important to cats, especially when they are living a more solitary life. Because they try to avoid fighting at all costs, they prioritize marking their turf with their scent as much as possible. This is fairly effective at keeping other cats away, as they are trying to avoid conflict themselves. When they do happen to find a strange cat on their territory, they will try to scare them off first. With the addition of various aggressive forms of body language, like an arched back and bristled fur to appear bigger, cats entail hostile vocalizations like growling and hissing in order to intimidate the stranger. Only if the attempt at scaring the intruder off doesn't work, do they resort to fighting.

Feral cat lands are actually laid out in a very specific and strategic way. At the very center is the core spot, where their den is typically located. This is where the cat goes to groom, eat, and sleep. Beyond this area is known as the hub of their territory. This is the part of their domain a cat will defend against other strays and keep marked heavily with their scent to protect from invasion. Next is the sector where the cat will hunt and explore throughout their active periods. Sometimes this zone of their territory will overlap with another cat's space. It forms a sort of neutral span where two strays may meet and peacefully interact.

Cat Colonies

Most cats tend to be fairly solitary, and your typical feline will not share their territory with another stray, except for in the instance that a female cat is nursing and raising kittens. However, depending on the environment they find themselves in, they have been known to form social groups, or colonies, under certain conditions. This willingness to form a pack will also depend on the personality of the cat. If they are more socially tolerant, they will be more inclined to enter into a larger colony. But socially intolerant cats are far less likely, even if the region is large and has an abundantly available source of food. While they can and will adapt to form social structures within these colonies, their groups don't exactly coexist or work together the way other packs of animals do. These social structures can exist in both the wild and within the homes of multi-cat families.

When cats do decide to live within a colony, they tend to follow a specifically matrilinear structure. This is built through the lineage of female descendants: These colonies are run by female cats and their kittens. While they have a rather rough form of hierarchy within their pack, it is not a strictly followed form of leadership. The relationship that these cats all share is more complex; Their interaction is more dependent upon the personal relationship between cats, including blood relation, their age, and their sex.

Those within these colonies will affiliate themselves with certain members within the pack over others, often tethered to these relationships. But because cats are solitary at their core, they don't form a similar mentality or structure the way that wild packs of dogs may. They still hunt alone and fend for themselves. The pack becomes less of a necessity for survival and more of a social group formed out of convenience and situational influence.

These colonies typically form in places with a surplus of food and shelter due to less of a need to fight over limited resources. It is possible for these cats to form fairly strong bonds between themselves and the cats they know well. This is especially true for the blood relationships shared between mother and kitten (or felines in the same litter).

An interesting common behaviour within these communities is for kittens to nurse from other females in the colony, even those that aren't producing milk. This behaviour probably helps to build social connections and relationships, thus leading to feeling more inclined to remain within the colony. Depending on the size of the territory that they live in, multiple colonies can form within the same area. There will be a larger, more central group that has the most control over food and other resources. The smaller groups that form around the central group will have available access to food, but they don't take priority. Typically cats in these groups are in poorer health or may be less likely to produce kittens.

So how do male cats fit into this structure? Adult males don't often live within the colonies, Instead live in their own domains, the outer parts of which could overlap with territories of multiple female-run communities. These single males will typically have larger territories than the packs: This could vary depending.on how big their colony is and how much food they can access. On average, their domains tend to be about three times larger than the territory of females. These could potentially end up being ten times larger, depending on various factors such as food density and female population. However, more dominant males tend to have larger lands, whereas more submissive males may have smaller ones. In these kinds of environments, it's not uncommon for male territories to overlap, though the odds are also influenced by prey availability and how many female colonies are within the area.

There is usually very little conflict within these communities themselves. Due to their social connections and familiarity with one another, they don't typically have a need or desire to fight amongst themselves. However, there is potential for conflict when male kittens reach sexual maturity. Once they hit that age, they are immediately excluded from the group and pushed to find their own territory to claim and hunt on.

Naturally, this process can trigger aggression between excluded males and the females of the colony. Another potential for conflict is between females and the local male cats when they run into each other on their lands. It's not often that the males will be aggressive toward females. When the female is not in heat she may act with hostility—if he gets too close to her or her territory. However, this isn't necessarily always the case. The two cats may greet one another and interact peacefully, including sniffing each other and rubbing their heads together. This is especially more common when two cats have some sort of familiarity with one another. Two male cats tend to interact fairly differently. They try to avoid one another altogether, or will only tolerate each other, but aren't typically friendly with one another. Aggression is possible between two male cats and is more likely than being between two females.

Because of their nature and lack of strict social hierarchies, cats don't have the more complex social signals other groups of wild animals have developed. Because of this, they typically are unable to signal with a sign of appeasement to each other. This causes aggression and conflict to easily escalate into a fight. This higher likelihood of fighting is why they try to avoid potential conflict or rely on intimidation first when around another aggressive cat.

So why is knowing about wild feline behaviour important to having a cat in your home? Well, for quite a few reasons! First, it's important to know that cats see your home, and thus where they live, as their territory. So it is likely they will feel inclined to mark the area as theirs and could potentially become hostile toward outsiders trying to enter the domain. This behaviour could potentially cause some issues when introducing another animal into the home.

However, if cat colonies are any indication, multiple cats can live peacefully in the home. It's important to keep in mind typical colony behaviour and, though it won't necessarily reflect exactly how things will work out, the typical social structure is a good guide for what kind of cat to bring into your home. But, we'll go over multi-cat homes, and how to introduce them to each other, in more detail in a later chapter!

Chapter 6: Eating and Drinking

Food and water are two of the biggest, and most basic, aspects of living and survival. We as humans have adapted our own methods of consuming these necessary things. But just like many other animals out there, cats have very different ways of handling them. As mentioned before, felines haven't evolved much past their basic instincts. A cat's intuition and their natural way of life remain closely related to their behaviour even now as fully domesticated cats. They are carnivorous hunters by nature. That means, despite them not necessarily hunting anything, a lot of their actions surrounding food and water still reflect those instincts.

Eating

Cats tend to have fairly interesting, and sometimes odd, eating behaviours. Many of them are rooted in their instincts or were learned environmentally as kittens. While cats tend to have personal tastes in terms of food flavor, many of their behaviours are commonly shared. For example, they are solitary hunters in the wild, and thus they tend to be solitary eaters. While they may occasionally share their food, most cats prefer to eat alone. If you find that your cat seems to be taking some food and going to eat elsewhere, it could be a sign that they aren't happy with the placement of their food bowl. You may need to move it to make their mealtimes more comfortable. Many cats, who hunt, prefer their prey fresh and at body temperature; Our house cats prefer the same temperature in their own food. This means it is important to ensure their food isn't too hot or too cold. Scratching around their bowls, or pulling things into them once finished, is a display of a typical habit. When hunting, if a cat had a meal they could not finish eating, it would 'save it for later' by scraping leaves over it. In the case of their food at home, they may attempt to bury their kibble, especially if given more food than they can eat in one sitting. The inclusion of meat is also an essential provision to guarantee a long healthy life. For this reason, it's crucial to follow a cat's diet requirements.

There are a few things to remember when deciding on the location of your cat's food. First and foremost, steer clear of putting it too close to their litter box. Not only is it unsanitary for them, but it's also in their nature to avoid eating near these areas for that reason. Secondly, bypass putting them in places too crowded or loud; These locations can discourage cats from eating due to being overwhelmed. This can be an even bigger issue if you have multiple cats. Try to put their bowls in places that are more calm and quiet. If you find your cat is nervous around others, it's a good idea to feed them in separate areas: having the space and quiet to enjoy their meal without added stress is best.

While many cats prefer to eat by themselves, some may even refuse to eat if around any other cat, a person, or loud and active noises. This activity or presence may make them feel unsafe. To combat this, try to feed your cat alone and in a very calm and quiet location. Make sure they feel safe enough to eat in peace. In addition, if you find that your cat has abruptly stopped eating, it's vitally important to figure out why. Have you changed their food recently? Is there something new or different in their environment that may be causing them stress or anxiety? Has there been any major change in their life or routine? If none of those things have happened, you should have your cat checked out by a vet as soon as possible. Even if there isn't anything seriously wrong, it's better to be safe than sorry; Cats can sometimes develop what is called fatty liver if they don't eat for too long. This condition can become very dangerous very quickly, so ensure that your cat is eating a consistent and healthy amount.

With that in mind, personal preference also heavily influences what kinds of food your cat will eat; But this can be impacted by the food they were introduced to as a kitten. For example, if they tried all types and textures when they were young, they are more likely to eat different foods as an adult. However, if only exposed to a couple types their entire lives, they may be less willing to try anything unfamiliar. It is also common for cats to grow bored of the food provided. They may stop eating their usual kibble and instead, seek out something new and interesting. This behaviour is normal by nature as it is a way to encourage eating a wide array of food to gain nutrients and dietary benefits. To avoid this causing health issues for your kitty, you should supplement their meal with variety. If you occasionally mix it up by giving them new kinds of foods and flavors, they will be less inclined to give up on their main food source.

Cats tend to only eat small meals, so it's not uncommon to see them taking a few bites from their bowl before returning to their other activities. While this may seem like your cat is unhappy with the food, that isn't necessarily the case. Their natural habits, paired with their smaller stomach, encourage them to eat small amounts throughout the day. Some cat owners will only feed their cats at specific times, often just twice in 24 hours. The problem with this is that it doesn't really reflect their natural eating habits. Wild cats frequently ingest during a 24-hour timeframe and they may even eat as many as 20 different times a day. Cats in homes that cannot keep food fresh and available all the time may overcompensate by eating a lot at each meal, which can cause discomfort and lead to health problems. If you have multiple cats in your home, a larger issue can develop due to competition over potentially limited resources.

In theory, feeding on demand is great, but typically ineffective; We normally sleep during the periods our cats are active. The most beneficial way to feed your cat is by providing free access to food. The initial reaction from owners tends to be that of concern for their cat's wellbeing. If my cat is allowed constant access to food, won't they become overweight? Because of their natural eating behaviours, they tend not to overeat on their own accord. But if this is a significant concern, cat owners can provide their cats with activity feeders; They not only make your cat work for their food but also control the portions. Handling cat obesity relies more on ensuring your cat is active and gets regular exercise rather than focusing on restricting their food intake. Some owners may not like this option; They may feel this process is less personal and takes away part of the caregiving process of having a pet. But cats don't get this kind of affection from food, so that really only benefits their human owners. In order to satisfy the wants and needs of both owner and pet, you can try hunting games. Essentially, you use a toy to engage with your cat and allow them to stalk, hunt, and pounce on it as if hunting prey in the wild. Afterward, you can reward their hunt with food. No matter what process you decide to do, you should always keep in mind the health and wellbeing of your cat. Some trial and error may be needed, but there are plenty of methods to practice and find what works best for both you and your kitty.

Many people tend to see feeding and eating as a social activity, and believe offering food to a cat denotes love and affection. Unfortunately, that isn't really the case when it comes to cats. They don't see eating as a social activity and only really approach it as a necessity to survival. Even cats who live in groups or colonies still tend to hunt, eat alone, and determine when to do so based on personal schedules. Their need for food is dictated by external factors, such as levels of light, time of day, and desire to hunt and eat over other potential motivations. While you may feel more inclined to view sharing a meal or treat in a social and caregiving manner, it's important to remember what is best for your cat's health and wellbeing.

Eating is an important part of every animal's health; It's important to watch out for any eating behaviours that could negatively affect your cat. Perhaps you find that they are gorging on food whenever they eat. Maybe try to feed them smaller meals more frequently during the day, or feed them in a more secluded and less stressful place. Doing this will ensure they don't feel pressured by other cats or animals to eat quickly. You may find that timed or activity feeders can slow down your cat's eating as well. If you find your cat enjoys swatting their food and spilling it before deciding to eat: They are simply following their predatory instincts. The fact they're actively enjoying the hunt is good; It may be a sign to invest in more toys and playtime to help your cat release pent-up hunting energy.

Drinking

Much like eating, cats can be very particular with their habits surrounding water; They have fairly specific tastes too. Cats often have preferences for where they want it, what kind it is, or even the dish type that contains it. While they may seem picky or finicky, it just takes a bit of time to get to know your pet's personal preferences.

There isn't a significant amount of research surrounding the drinking behaviour of cats compared to other fields of study. Such that, some of the information we do have is skeptical at best. For example, it is known that individual species of animals evolve differently depending on their environment and the general natural order of things. When it comes to domestic cats: We discovered evolution granted them the ability to handle significant loss in fluids—They conserve what remains by producing concentrated urine. There is speculation that this is because modern domestic cats descended from desert-dwelling wildcats that needed the ability to preserve water in a dry environment.

Moreover, while we don't know why or if these evolutionary behaviours play a hand in it, cats are predisposed to certain health conditions. Things such as kidney problems and urinary tract infections are common among domesticated cats. These behaviours may cause damage over time, which is less likely for wild cats, and more of a problem for domestic cats with significantly longer life expectancies. Because domestic cats get less exercise and are fed instead of hunting, living within domestic conditions potentially increases the risk. The truth is: We don't know the exact cause. But we do know that monitoring the fluid intake of your cat is vital.

When it comes to wild cats, they tend to get most of their required water intake simply from hunting and eating their prey. Because most prey consumed carries about 70% moisture, acquiring the necessary daily food intake covers most, if not all, fluid concerns as well. If your cat eats dry food, they are only ingesting about 10% of their water intake and thus must get a higher amount of water from other sources. It is recommended cats be fed wet food, or a mixture of wet and dry, in order to up their water intake through food consumption. But this doesn't cover all of their needs, so continue to provide access to other sources.

If you can, you should set up multiple spots for your cat to drink. They should be placed in different rooms and away from where your cat eats. Doing this will encourage your cat to drink water no matter where they're at during the day. But it also gives them access to water should something prevent them from approaching a specific bowl (another cat's presence, other external factors, or stressors). When setting up these bowls, be sure they aren't too close to their food or the litter box. Cats tend to avoid water nearby these locations as they can be contaminated. If you catch your cat frequently trying to drink from your glass of water, this is a sign they need access to more or fresher water.

Now comes the task of finding out how your cat likes their water. When picking the bowls used, the material doesn't seem to matter much outside of personal preference.

Metal, glass, ceramic, and plastic are all fine; Your cat may just prefer one material over the other. However, there is a consensus among cats that they seem to prefer smaller bowls. When setting up throughout your house, try to use different materials and slightly different sizes, especially if you have multiple cats. This will help you get to know your cat's personal preferences and satiate the various tastes should your home be a multi-cat one. No matter what kind of bowl you settle on, make sure you're checking them frequently and refilling them with fresh water. You also want to ensure that the bowls are getting cleaned each day. Doing so with dish soap or a dishwasher is fine, but do not use disinfectants, as this can be toxic. Checking and cleaning it each day will ensure your cat always has access to clean and fresh water. Some may also prefer the running water of a cat fountain, which could be a nice alternative. However, much like the material of their bowls, cats will be drawn to either option simply due to personal taste. While many cats enjoy running water, some cats become distressed by water fountains. At the end of the day, the type of receptacle will rely on their overall preference. So try a few different choices and see what option calls to them.

Tap water is typically fine to give your cats. However, if you notice that yours has an odd smell or is heavily chlorinated, you should opt for filtered water. This can be via a filter added at the water source or by giving your pet non-carbonated mineral water. Providing them rainwater is a choice as well; Some cats tend to prefer more freshwater.

If your cat has outside access, then it may be more inclined to drink from an outdoor receptacle. This could be anything from puddles, ponds, and flowerpots to fountains, watering cans, and anything that collects rainwater. Although they may prefer this option, be sure to keep indoor dishes available. This is good practice since they could lose access to an outdoor source at any point. In addition, while this is typically fine, you should check that your cat isn't drinking from anything potentially toxic. Fountains, for example, may have chemicals in them; There could also be pesticides in flowerpots. Likewise, ensure not to use any dangerous chemicals within water sources they may find tempting to drink. This is important for indoor use as well. Cats are known to lick faucets, sink, and bathtub drains, etcetera. Always rinse these areas thoroughly after bathing to prevent your feline from becoming ill. Equally important, your cat should not have access to chemically cleaned water sources, such as toilets. Last but not least, don't leave potentially dangerous drinks around, such as coffee or soda. Any chemical that a cat ingests could be fatal for your kitty. Always be diligent in providing proper water resources.

Chapter 7: Cat Sleeping Habits

Cats sleep a lot. Even people who have never owned one know that. But the issue comes when people assume that their sleeping habits mean that they are lazy or inactive. This is far from the case. Cats are incredibly active animals anytime that they are awake. Because of their natural instincts as hunters, their sleeping patterns connect deeply with their nature as wild cats. So when you keep finding your kitty curled up somewhere comfy or in a patch of sunlight snoozing the day away, remember that it's innately in their nature. The cuteness overload is just a bonus.

Typically cats will sleep for around 12 to 16 hours a day, and that number only increases as they get older. Kittens also tend to sleep more frequently, and they can be pretty heavy sleepers when worn out! Due to their natural hunting instincts, they tend to be most active around dawn and dusk (which happens to be when their prey is out). To conserve as much energy as they can, cats will sleep throughout the day. Doing so allows them to remain active and hunt as much prey as possible once dusk arrives. This entire sleep cycle is driven by instinct. Wild cats, during the day, would find places to hide and rest to avoid predators and prepare for their evening hunt. This instinct also means the weather can influence their sleep schedule; On cold and rainy days, your cat is sometimes even sleepier than usual. Since cats are fairly adaptive creatures, over time you may notice your pet has adjusted its sleep schedule slightly to mirror yours. This allows them to be more awake and active the same hours that you're home. Which means more playtime and affection!

Despite how often cats sleep, there are several similarities between their sleeping patterns and those of humans. For example, both experience a REM (rapid eye movement) cycle of sleep. This sleep is typically very heavy and indicated by the movement of the eyes underneath closed lids accompanied by deeper breathing. Cats also have similar non-REM sleep cycles to humans. These cycles range from light to deep sleep. You may notice that your cat is napping somewhere, but the smallest movement or sound causes them to jump up from their spot. While other times, it may take a bit more effort to rouse your sleeping companion. This is an indication of which kind of sleep your kitty was experiencing before awakening.

Again like humans, cats are affected by circadian rhythms. This is, essentially, your inner clock which tells you when to awake and sleep. It works on a 24 hour cycle and affects how your body is functioning throughout the day. Our circadian rhythm tells us to be awake during the day and asleep at night.

However, the one your cat operates on tells them to be awake around dusk and dawn and to be asleep at night and during the day. We've talked about this point a few times before, as this behaviour heavily impacts several aspects of your cat's daily life. The awake periods are affected by the intervals of time when prey would typically be active. Their sleeping periods: influenced by when predators are more likely to be active, as well as energy conservation.

You may find that your cat enjoys sleeping on or around you, or even on your bed when you aren't in it. This could be a sign that they are comfortable around you and trust you, or they could be seeking out the warmth of your body heat. The process also mingles your scent with your cat's scent, which could bring a sense of comfort to your kitty while they sleep. Sleeping with them can also help to strengthen your bond. However, some people may find this difficult due to their different sleeping patterns. Allowing them to sleep with you at night will take some adaptation and personal preference.

Do Cats Dream?

So, if our cats have such a similar sleep pattern to us, does that mean they dream as well? Of course, there's no real way to know for certain. We can't exactly ask our cats if they're dreaming or what about. But, there are a few different behaviours that indicate cats likely experience dreams. They will sometimes twitch, kick, or even make vocal noises in deep sleep; Many experts and researchers believe this is a sign they are dreaming. But what could our cats possibly be dreaming of? Much like us humans, and most other animals, they likely dream about their everyday experiences. Hunting, playing, and exploring, are just a few examples of what they could be seeing in their feline dreams. They may even dream of their favorite human companions. Knowing this also means they may experience nightmares as well.

Chapter 8: Interacting With Other Animals

Cats are typically very solitary animals but proven to be adaptable to social structures when given the right environment. When living in homes with their human companions, they have adapted to and can form close bonds with their owners after spending significant time together. By now, you should have a pretty good understanding of a cat's behaviour around its owners. But what about other cats, or even dogs? While homes exist with multiple cats living comfortably together, or even felines and canines cohabiting in harmony, it's not as simple as having them in the same house. The general nature of cats heavily influences how they interact with other animals. So let's take a moment to talk about the typical social behaviour they exhibit around them.

Cat Social Interactions

When it comes to communicating with one another, cats tend to use more subtle movements; These can be so brief that you may not see or notice them. As mentioned before, cats are not overtly expressive, so their method of interacting with cats, other animals, or even humans is simple. Paying close attention to your cat and being aware of what to look out for is the key to recognizing and interpreting this behaviour.

Cats don't tend to rely on vocal communication when they are interacting with other cats. They rarely meow at one another and tend to devote that interaction to their human companions. That isn't to say that they never 'speak' to one another. They do tend to trill or chirp at other cats but are typically more vocal when trying to communicate with their owners. Cats will purr when in contact with other cats, however depending on the other clues in this interaction, that could be positive or negative. Remember to look for those non-verbal cues to tell if the situation is comfortable or tense. While they may not often meow back and forth, as we've covered earlier, cats won't hesitate to express their anger or aggression toward one another.

The body language we discussed is vital to figuring out what your cat is feeling—including when interacting with others. If they approach another cat with more happy and positive cues, they feel confident and comfortable around them. Cats may also make eye contact with each other. If they blink slowly at one another, they are happy approaching and interacting with the other feline in their immediate vicinity. Sometimes, however, they may feel nervous around the other cat and show their more skittish and anxious cues. They may even seem slow or hesitant to approach. If your cat looks away or starts to lick their lips, they feel threatened or uncomfortable with the other cat. Be careful! Interactions between cats could quickly spiral into aggression—Look out for those more subtle cues that indicate a rise in anger.

Cats that are comfortable around one another will often greet each other or communicate through physical contact. They may bump their heads together or rub their bodies against one another as a form of greeting. This action is more than just a simple physical contact between the two cats, however. As we've covered extensively in a previous chapter, smells and their scenting abilities are vital to how cats interact with the world around them. When rubbing against a familiar cat, they are doing two things. Firstly, they are rubbing their scent on the other cat, which is considered a friendly behaviour between two cats and can be seen as affectionate. They are also picking up the smell of the other cat. Having this scent from the greeting allows them to know more about the other cat, and that can assist in deciding how to handle the interaction past that point.

Having a Multi-Cat Home

It's probably a very tempting idea—adopting another feline—Once you have one cat, the desire to bring another one into the mix is almost unbearable. Having another one in your home could indeed benefit both you and your first kitty. But it is not a decision that should be made on a whim; Nor is it a process to be done abruptly. Even if you see an irresistibly cute little kitten you want to bring home. There are several things to consider and steps you should take when introducing another cat into your family.

Before deciding to get another feline, you should consider the personality and state of your current one. If they are still fairly young and playful, then a new kitten should be no issue. But if they are older and frailer, getting a more mature and calm companion may be a better idea. Overall just try to look for personalities that could match well with the identity of the cat you already have at home. You should also take into account their age and sex. Typically the best idea is to get one who is younger than your cat, fixed, and of the opposite sex, so there is less chance of them competing with one another in some way.

With that in mind, you should make certain to prioritize the health and wellbeing of your first cat when you are considering another one. Make sure that they are physically healthy and up to date on their shots and checkups with your vet. You also want to keep an eye on their emotional health and ensure that they feel comfortable, safe, and happy in their environment. If they are experiencing other stressors, adding another cat into the mix could only worsen their behaviour.

Not every cat will be pleased with another feline in their space. If yours displays fear or aggression toward ones that visit your yard, they likely won't take to a new cat within their territory. However, if they seem more curious toward other cats, it may not trigger that many negative emotions for your kitty. It may be disappointing to realize that your cat won't tolerate another cat in your home, but their wellbeing should be your priority.

If you conclude that your current cat could handle, and potentially enjoy, a new companion then, it's time to introduce them to one another. As emphasized before, changes to their environment and routine can throw them off significantly. And now you have two cats who are about to experience changes to their environments! The best way to handle introducing them to one another is to do so at a slow pace so that they both are as comfortable as possible.

A good start to this process is to try and introduce the two cats to one another's scent immediately. We talked at length about how important smells are to them and how they use their senses to communicate and recognise other cats. If you can manage to let both of them be exposed to one another's scent first, you can give them a head start on this recognition process.

The next step is to set up a space for your new cat. This will be their 'territory' as they become adapted to their new home. While it should be closed off from your other cat, the two should still be able to smell one another from under a door. Make sure this room has everything your new kitty needs, such as food and water, a litter box, and plenty of toys to keep them entertained. You also want to ensure that the people in your house can access the room easily. This will allow the new cat to get love and attention from everyone while staying in there during the acclimation process.

Before you start introducing them, you should try feeding both cats on either side of the door. Doing so will help them associate something positive, such as their food, with one another. Try to be patient, as this will take some time. If the two show aggression or hostility toward one another, then you should stop and hold off physically introducing them. Wait until mealtimes become peaceful before taking the next step of introduction. Next, the two should switch spaces. Place your first cat in the room for a few days while the new one is granted access to the rest of the house. This allows both of them to be exposed to each other's scent again, and it gives your new kitty the ability to explore their new home. You should also continue feeding them at the door.

After letting a few days pass and allowing both cats to get used to the new smells and environments, you should allow them to have visual contact. Now open the door, but place a pet gate between them. They will be able to see, smell, and interact with one another, but without having complete physical contact just yet.

The final step to the introduction is to remove the gate and let them freely meet and socialize! You'll want to keep a close eye on their behaviour and ensure that there isn't any significant hostility. Some conflict may be possible, but if it escalates or continues for a prolonged amount of time, you will need to separate them again. You should not leave them alone together in these earlier stages, especially if there is some tension between them. Keep them in their separate environments when you aren't around until you feel like they are interacting with each other in a normal and peaceful manner. If they are showing these positive signs, then they can be alone for longer periods. This process may take a significant amount of time and patience, but it is worth it in the end.

The method we have gone over is the most ideal path to take. However, it may not always be possible. Maybe you don't have the space to set up a whole separate room for your new cat, or you have very suddenly become the owner of one due to a surprise circumstance. This technique, luckily, can be altered to fit whatever situation you are in. Just remember that it should be a process. Do not just throw two cats together and expect them to work it out. Even if you can't follow it strictly, you should keep the introduction process in mind when bringing a new cat into the home. Skipping the whole thing can cause serious behaviour problems and could potentially end in conflict, aggression, and injuries.

Next, if you have multiple cats in your home already, it's time to make sure that they have more than enough of their necessities, as well as easy access to them. Confirm that you are feeding them out of separate bowls. Having them share a community food source can cause problems between them which can escalate to aggression. Separating the food allows them both to feel comfortable eating without the potential threat of another cat stealing it. As mentioned in chapter six, remember to have plenty of spots for both of them to have water! Not only that, but you also want to make sure there are enough litter boxes to go around. The typical rule is to have one litter box per cat and then an extra one. This method ensures there are plenty of spaces for everyone to use the bathroom and prevents potential territorial disputes.

Secondly, both cats should have access to more than enough scratching posts and a wide variety of toys for them to use—They shouldn't feel like they have to fight over things like this at any point. Make sure that they both get enough of you too! You should be dedicating specific attention and playtime to both of the cats in your house; Neither should feel like the other is getting more of your undivided attention.

Make sure that you keep an eye on their relationship and how they interact with one another. They may be peaceful now, but over time, this could justifiably shift. While potentially caused by a variety of things, including health problems or external factors, you want to make sure that it doesn't escalate into anything possibly dangerous. Keeping both cats in a stable, enriching environment will keep them happy and healthy. And will cut back on any possibility for tension.

Don't allow either of the cats to bully one another. Play fighting is one thing and is a rather common behaviour, but make sure you are reading the body language of both of them. If one of them is being pounced on and seems distressed or upset, or the one doing it is being more aggressive than necessary, it's time to step in and stop the conflict. If you notice tension developing between the two or see that they appear to be gearing up for a fight, stop them before they can follow through. Just make sure that you are incredibly careful not to catch a stray claw in the process. To keep a good peace in your newly made multi-cat home, you want to make sure that both have plenty of personal space. What this could mean may depend on your cat. Some may be more tolerable and could only require a perch or a comfy spot away from the other for a brief time. Other cats may need a whole separate room that is theirs alone and that your other kitty can't set a paw in. You need to figure out what works best for you and your cats and how to make them both comfortable in their home.

Cats and Dogs

There is a common perception in popular media that depicts dogs and cats as mortal enemies. From cartoons to your favorite movies, dogs are often shown as being unable to resist chasing after cats, even breaking free from owners to tear after them; Cats are depicted as loving to taunt and trick dogs, even leading them into traps or other predicaments. However, despite this, they can get along. But this relies rather heavily on the personality of both animals. Not all of them will mesh well, and some homes with both animals are not exactly healthy or stable for either animal. So why is it that these two pet types appear unable to live with one another peacefully?

When it comes to housing two cats together, it is a lot easier since the two share similarities in behaviour and overall body language. But cats and dogs can be much more difficult; The two animals don't exactly see things the same way, nor do they express emotions the same. To begin with, some of their vocalizations don't exactly translate properly when they try to communicate with one another. Things like barking, meowing, and purring seem to just be noises to either animal and not something that the other can understand. Another thing is tail movements. When a dog is excited, they will often wag their tail to show their happiness. But to a cat, this may appear as more aggressive behaviour, and they may take it as a negative sign. This could cause them to become defensive.

The two animals also have a bit of trouble greeting one another, as dogs tend to go straight for a sniff while cats will try to bump heads as a sign of greeting. It can be a bit confusing to both animals as neither will really take the other's action as welcoming. When a dog goes to raise their paw, they are looking to play, while when a cat does the same, they are giving a warning sign before they strike. Unfortunately, the two very different emotions can lead to confusion and potentially a whimpering pup. Both animals have rather expressive ears, and while we have gone over a cat's body language extensively, a dog does not move their ears in the same manner. For example, they tend to hold their ears forward as a sign of aggression and have them pulled back to show they are fearful: To cats, forward and alert ears are a positive sign, and ears that are folded back are seen as aggressive. These nearly opposite expressions could cause either animal to misread the body language of the other: Which can end in potential conflict.

Despite there sometimes being miscommunication between them, there are plenty of households where cats and dogs live in harmony. This may be due to some aspects of communication that the two animals can share, even if other things are a bit difficult. One example is their eyes. Much like cats, dogs will often blink slowly to show affection, or they will stare rather intensely as a sign of aggression or a threat. They can also look at one another's mouths, as both will draw back their lips and show their teeth as a threat or a warning for another animal to back off. In addition, there are certain vocalizations that the two animals share, such as shrieking and growling. Since both animals can make these noises and have a rather similar concept of them, they can pick up on the fear, pain, and aggression behind these sounds.

As mentioned before, the compatibility of specific cats and dogs will depend heavily on personality and environment. You may have a pair that hit it off great and even play together, or you may have ones that get into spats or terrorize one another. Should you decide to have a dog and a cat in the same home, make sure that you introduce them slowly, similar to how you would two cats. It may not take the same process, but the feline of the house will need time to adjust to the new roommate just the same. Also, make sure that your cat still has a safe place to go to have time away from the dog. This will often mean a place high enough that they can't reach or a space that the dog cannot access. You should include your cat's items in these areas: such as their food and water bowls, their litter box, and their toys. They may tolerate, and even occasionally enjoy, the dog's presence, but that does not mean they have any interest in sharing their stuff with them. Especially since cats need their own spaces to feel safe and comfortable, make sure they always have access to an area like this where they can be alone. Keeping their food and litter box away from the dog is good practice. It allows your cat to eat and do its business without being interrupted or feeling threatened by another presence. And it keeps the pup from snacking on your kitty's food and excrement.

Even if the two can't communicate completely, it is possible to have a cat and dog in the same home living happily and peacefully. Seeing them groom one another or nap together are probably some of the best signs of this. Grooming is a vitally social activity for cats: Grooming your dog is an indication that they have accepted them as part of their family. Sleeping together shows that the two animals are comfortable enough around one another to be vulnerable and at a disadvantage. So your cat, in that particular moment, doesn't feel defensive or aggressive toward the dog. While they may not always be peaceful, so long as you keep your home stable and safe for both animals, you can still have a happy fur baby family.

Keeping Small Animals Around

While two of the more common animals: Cats and dogs aren't always the only pets people have at home. Hamsters, birds, bunnies, and fish are just a few of the smaller animals that some people also own. If you plan to add both a cat and a smaller animal to your family, there are quite a few things to remember before making the decision. First and foremost: They are hunters, so you should consider that bringing this small animal into your home could look like an easy meal for your kitty. It is possible to have them in the same house, but you are still running that potential risk of feline instincts taking over.

While birds make lovely pets and owners enjoy their chirping sounds and songs, so do felines. Birds are not always a good fit for homes with a cat due to the fact their natural behaviours set off a cat's predatory radar sensors. Even if they are safely inside of their cages, they may become subject to the hunting behaviours of their housemate. Smaller birds could be scared into a heart attack. They may even pluck their feathers or refuse to eat due to the stress. Even the larger bird breeds wouldn't do well around cats for a few reasons. Many of them require time outside of their cages, which leaves them easily accessible to the quick reflexes of your cat. Not to mention birds are notably fragile. A simple bite or scratch could seriously harm or kill them. If you already own a bird and plan to get a cat or the other way round, you should make this choice very carefully. While not an impossible task, understanding the needs of both your feline and feathery friends is important when choosing to add them to the same family unit.

Rodents, such as mice, hamsters, gerbils, rats, and guinea pigs, should be kept as separated from your cat as possible. Their cage should be secure enough that the rodent can't escape, and the kitty can't get a paw in. Cat's can pull off the plastic tops of containers with twist lids, so simply keeping a lid on the enclosure won't work. It should also be entirely out of their reach. If you place it somewhere high up, there is still a chance that your cat may try to get to them. This could result in a habitat knocked to the floor. If possible, keep the cage in a room where your cats aren't allowed inside. This is the best way to ensure their safety. Do not try to integrate the animals. Even if you think your cat couldn't hurt a fly: that simply isn't true. They are hunters by nature; Their instincts can easily kick in when they spot a prey animal. Also, the rodent may instinctually defend itself by biting your cat. If you have let the rodent out of the cage to run about and explore, do not leave them completely unsupervised. There are plastic balls you can place your small critter in for exercise. Put them inside it on the floor in a room with the door shut while they enjoy their safe little bubble. No felines should be allowed in the room even if they are inside the ball. It could stress out your tiny pet and potentially cause your kitty to give chase.

Rabbits are one of those animals that are a bit more likely to get along with your cat. However, similarly to with other cats and dogs, you will have to introduce the two animals to each other slowly. Rabbits are more authoritative and confrontational; If they are confident and comfortable in their space, they will be more likely to challenge a prowling cat. Standing up to them can sometimes cause your kitty to back down. Rabbits need a much larger cage as well, so you'll want to have this set up somewhere that is safely away from feline paws. You don't want them to feel cornered or stressed in this situation. Rabbits are delicate and could potentially suffer heart attacks from too much stress. However, over time the two animals can become comfortable with one another and can even be friends! But that doesn't mean you should leave them alone or let the rabbit wander freely without supervision. Even if they are friendly, your cat is still a hunter. One incident can trigger their desire to pounce. Always be present if the two pets are interacting.

Similarly, ferrets can get along with cats successfully. Since they are also hunters, they can hold their own should they need to do so when interacting with a feline. However, your cat will always have the upper paw in any sort of confrontation—They're simply bigger and stronger. Due to this, it's best to handle them similarly to how you would handle rabbits. Make sure that both animals have their own space and toys so that there is less of a chance for conflict. Both should be getting plenty of your undivided attention as well. But again, one thing is vital to remember: Don't leave them alone without any supervision. This has been a fairly common theme when discussing smaller animals, but it's not without reason. If a conflict arises or your cat misreads a playful bounce, your ferret could be seriously harmed.

Fish are another prime example, as they can become fairly stressed by the presence of your cat. It's a bit unfortunate, as they tend to enjoy sitting and watching their aquatic friends. The best way to have both animals happy is to train your kitty not to get too close to the tank. Make sure you don't keep a table or chair next to their tank either. Those spots give them easy access to spring right on top of the lid. You can also cover the top with textures that your cat dislikes to discourage them from getting up there. Should you manage to keep them from harassing your poor fish, then they may be able to live peacefully together. Fish are a bit easier to have with cats if you happen to own a fairly large tank inset into a wall within your home. Since the access point of these tanks tend to be hidden and out of reach, they are the safest option when a feline friend is involved. However, if a smaller tank is more your speed, there is still the option to place the tank in a room out of your cat's reach.

If you decide to have a small animal and a cat within the same home despite the risks, remember that your vigilance and awareness are the most important factors in keeping them safe. You should also ensure that you are keeping an eye on the well-being of both your pets. If they are displaying signs of stress, you may need to reevaluate the living situation. The health of your animals is a priority when deciding on whether or not you can own a smaller animal alongside your cat; You must be entirely certain of that choice. Just because they are caged animals does not mean that their wellness is easily dismissed as less important.

Chapter 9: Training Unwanted Behaviours

There's a rather common misconception that cats are untrainable. Due to them being famous for their independence and strong will, some people believe that cats are just too stubborn to be taught anything in the way that dogs can: But that would actually be far from the case. Training takes time and patience but is strongly recommended. Even though most cat owners won't be teaching them to perform entertaining tricks, training is still an important part of having a comfortable and stress-free environment. Cats will likely get into trouble when first acclimating to your home because they don't know what they are, or aren't, allowed to do or where. They have their needs, desires, and normal behaviours that they pursue, and they don't see objects and environments the same way that humans do. They have a need to mark their territory so that other cats know what belongs to them, so they scratch surfaces in the most frequented areas in the home (often causing them to tear up couches and beds). Or your cat simply wants to get a higher vantage point over their territory, so they choose to jump onto your counters or shelves, often knocking things over in the process. Despite these behaviours, and many more, being natural and beneficial to them, they can lead to frustration and expenses. So be sure to teach your cat where they are and aren't allowed early on in the process.

That being said, it's important to remember that you

cannot simply stop your cat from doing these things. Oftentimes these behaviours are rooted in their natural instincts. So training turns more into correction and redirection and becomes less focused on complete alteration. One of the biggest key parts of being able to correct your cat's misbehaviours is, of course, recognizing their normal, natural habits. Having a good grasp on why your cat acts in a particular way will help you understand how to train and correct the behaviour: This will benefit you both. Not only will you be more successful, but it will be far less frustrating for you and your cat.

However, before you begin training any sort of behaviour out of your cat, you should first determine if something else could be causing the negative conduct. Two of the biggest possibilities are that something is physically wrong with them or some sort of environmental factor has triggered the misbehaviour. These are especially true if the action has started rather abruptly.

Cats can only communicate with us in very limited ways. On top of that, they try to hide the fact that something is wrong with them. If they were to appear weak or injured in the wild, then they would become easy targets for predators. So shifts in behaviour, even mere minor ones, are the most telling sign that something is wrong. If you are ever in doubt, you should opt to take your pet to see the vet, even if you aren't entirely sure that something is wrong. After all, it's better to be safe than sorry.

If there is nothing wrong medically, then you should next turn to their environment. Cats are animals that thrive on routine and stability: Although they are adaptable over time, sudden and severe shifts in their schedule or their territory can throw them off and make them stressed, anxious, or even aggressive.

New animals or people in their environment, major moves in location, or even shifts in your routine, such as a change in job or schooling, can all cause your cat stress. This stress can trigger a multitude of negative behaviours including marking things with urine or scratching, aggression or fear directed at the new animal or person, and even behaviours such as excessive grooming or chewing that can end up harming them physically.

Whenever possible, try to introduce these changes slowly and over a longer period. This will allow them to adjust easier to changes in the environment and when establishing a new routine.

However, this may not always be possible. Life can be unpredictable and things may have to change suddenly. If that's the case, ensure that you give your cat a safe and comfortable area to go to when they're feeling stressed. You should also try and keep things as close to their normal routine as possible. Things like feeding time or playtime should remain the same so that your cat still has a bit of their routine that hasn't changed. If neither health nor outside stressors seem to be causing their misbehaviours, then it's time to learn the best ways to train them.

Common Misbehaviours and How to Correct Them

While every cat is different, there are quite a few commonplace problem habits for all cat owners. This list is far from comprehensive, but it does touch on several of the more frequently seen misbehaviours. Certain training techniques tend to be more helpful with very specific behaviours. But there are plenty of methods we will be covering that could help correct other unwanted conduct. So, let's dive in and discuss what's possible to help train these bad habits out of your cat.

Aggression

If your cat becomes suddenly aggressive, it is likely due to an environmental cause or for health reasons. Aggression doesn't come from just anywhere, so it's likely something triggered it, especially if your cat has never shown it before. Take a moment to assess their environment or routine and ensure nothing major has changed to cause the shift. New pets or people in their environment, or significant changes to their routine, can cause your cat to become stressed and act out. It's important to handle these things slowly and delicately, whenever possible, to avoid your cat reacting negatively. If nothing has changed in their environment and the aggression seems to have come out of nowhere, then you should take your pet to the vet to get them looked over. It could be stemming from an illness or injury, and they have no other way to express that they're hurt or uncomfortable.

Hyperactivity

Cats, especially younger ones and kittens, can have a lot of energy. They may spend bouts of time running around, pouncing on things, and attacking and playing with toys or other cats. If they have too much energy or become bored, they can become destructive and develop bad habits. The best way to avoid this is to ensure that your cat has more than enough entertainment and stimulation within your home. Make sure they have access to a variety of toys from which to choose. You should also devote periods of your own time to play with your cat. Even 15 to 30 minute periods of play can help tire your pet out, keep them entertained, and also active. There are all kinds of toys you can use for this; Those include dangling toys, laser pointers, or even balls or mouse toys. Take the time to try out different ones with your cat and see which one is their favorite. Also, try to mix it up so that they don't get bored with their toys. To repeat, not only will actively playing with your pet help tire them out and keep their energy in check but—it will also help to strengthen the bond between you both! Plus it's just a lot of fun to watch your furry companion play!

Rough Play Sessions

Another issue often seen when it comes to cat playtime is aggressive cat play. If you find that your cat is directing their claws and teeth toward you when they're playing, or they get a bit out of hand, don't take this as them attacking you to hurt you. They're just wanting to play, but they see you as a fellow cat; They don't understand that their claws hurt your skin much more than it would another cat's fluffy pelt.

As mentioned before, try to dedicate several windows of time where you actively play with your cat. Doing so will not only tire them out but discourage them from bothering you and asking to play when you just want to relax or rest. Make sure to offer them a variety of toys, including ones that they can stalk and pounce on to satisfy their need to hunt and kill prey. Toys that they can bite, wrestle with, and kick are also a good idea.

If you regularly leave your home for several hours a day, ensure that your home is set up to keep your cat entertained and enriched. If they spend all day napping while you're gone then they're going to be excited and ready to play the moment you return home, while you may be more interested in resting for a while. That can be frustrating for you both. Things such as feeding puzzles or toys that are battery operated can help to entertain and tire out your cat while you are away.

It would also be a good idea to give them new and exciting toys to investigate from time to time. Doing so will keep them from getting too bored. When interacting with your pet, make sure to keep an eye on their body language. Give them attention and affection when they're seeking it, but not when they're in a playful mood, or they may be inclined to use that high energy on you. When playing with your cat, try not to use your hands or feet during playtime. Doing so will encourage them to target you when it is not playtime, which can cause you both injury and frustration. Don't let your cat equate you to a toy and instead focus their attention on their actual toys.

Another way to handle aggression during playtime is to simply ignore them. Say you're trying to play with them, but they start targeting you or acting too aggressive. This method involves you completely removing your attention from them, going so far as to leave the room to show that the behaviour is not acceptable. Don't touch or acknowledge them in any way until they have calmed down. They will likely be upset about the sudden ending to their play session and will associate that with the negative behaviour.

Once they seem to have calmed, you can resume the attention. You can also try giving them a large toy that they can kick and bite to release some of that pent-up energy. Sprinkling catnip on it as a bonus will not only attract them to it but also help them calm down after their play session.

Scratching Furniture

As mentioned before, cats are compelled to mark their territory with their scent and claw marks. This could lead to them potentially damaging surfaces that you don't want to be torn by their scratching. The first step in preventing this behaviour is ensuring you have plenty of surfaces in your home that your cat is allowed to claw on. Make sure that your kitty has more than enough scratching posts that they can use. Also, try putting these posts in the places that you and your cat frequent the most.

One of the main reasons your cat may be scratching things such as the couches and your bed is because they smell strongly of you! So putting scratching posts in the more communal areas will help to encourage them to use their claws on the permitted surfaces instead. Also, if you have a kitty who enjoys catnip, take some and sprinkle it onto the scratching post. This action will attract your cat to it— Distraction complete! This is a really simple trick to keep your belongings safe from scratches.

No matter how frustrating it becomes or how impatient you get, you should never consider declawing your cat. This practice is dangerous for them and is also terrible for their health. Declawing causes them serious physical, mental, and emotional problems. Pain, infection, sensitivity in the paws, and tissue death are just some of the issues that your cat can develop should you choose to get them declawed. This can, in turn, cause them to pick up even more serious behavioural problems than the ones you were trying to correct. It's better to devote your time to training the habit out of your cat than to sentence them to the trauma and pain that the procedure causes.

Eating Plants

Some cats seem to find enjoyment in chewing on any plants they can get their teeth on. Whether they do it because they like the taste or texture (or if they're just bored) this could be potentially dangerous if you aren't careful about keeping an eye on them. If your cat starts eating any of the plants and flowers you have around the house, then you should make a major effort to try and curb this immediately. While most cats are often deterred by plants toxic to them, that is not always the case with others. It's important to monitor or remove plants you don't want your cat accidentally ingesting if it could be dangerous.

First and foremost, you should make sure that any plants and flowers you bring into your house, especially those that your pet could decide to chew on, are not dangerous to them. If you are already being extra safe when it comes to what you bring into your home, then your next biggest concern is probably the wellbeing of your poor plant. Try to keep any that you don't want your cat eating in a high enough place, or in spots where they have no way to gain access to it. You could also try to redirect their attention from the plant and onto something else. You could use a toy or even a treat to try and distract them so that their focus is no longer on the plant. Make sure you repeat this process until they lose complete interest in it. Alternatively, if your cat is very adamant about eating your plants, you could consider buying cat-safe ones. An example is cat grass, which they would be allowed to chew on and eat. If you decide to go that route, it is important that you still ensure your cat is not eating too much of the plants and that you consult your veterinarian if you are unsure about your pet's diet or if it would be healthy for them.

Destructive Chewing

Aside from trying to eat plants, you may find that your cat has started chewing on other objects. This could be anything from your furniture and clothing to the cords on your electronic devices. Not only can this be damaging but also very frustrating and expensive to replace. It's important to rule out any potential health issues first when addressing a destructive chewer. A cat with tooth pain, gum disease, or one that was weaned too early could all be chewing to cope with pain or as a method of self-soothing. Like with any potential health cause, you should get your pet checked out by a vet before starting to alter the behaviour. If that is ruled out, then there are a few ways to help curb their chewing. Some cats will chew on things purely out of boredom, so you want to make sure that your kitty has more than enough toys and other objects that they are allowed to chew on and with which to play. If they seem to like chewing on furniture, or items that have a softer texture, try and entice them with toys that have a similarly soft feel to them. Diverting their attention to these toys will help them lose interest in the objects you don't want them chewing on. If they are chewing on wires, try to hide them as much as possible so that they don't have or can't gain access to them. This is not always plausible, as a lot of areas, such as around computers or televisions, may have several cords gathered in one place that can't be hidden easily. To discourage your cat from chewing on them, try using material such as double-sided tape on the ground around the wires. Cats dislike touching this texture with their paws, and they will be far less inclined to go near the cords.

Climbing on Surfaces

Cats enjoy being able to climb onto higher surfaces and having a better view of their territory, and sometimes that means getting onto your shelves or kitchen counters. This can be frustrating because it is unsanitary and gives your pet access to potentially fragile things for them to knock over. One way to discourage them from this is to give them access to raised surfaces and vantage points that they are allowed to climb. Things such as cat trees or shelves will allow them to get to a higher point without putting your fragile knick-knacks at risk. Similar to the scratching posts, you should put these in the communal areas, so they're still able to be around you and look down upon their favorite places. You can also deter your cats from getting on surfaces you don't want them on by covering the surface with things that have textures cats dislike. Aluminum foil and sticky paper are effective for this, as cats don't like to put their paws on it; It will discourage them from getting on the surface you have it on. Another good way to get them off of surfaces is by using sound. Producing a loud noise, such as clapping, can startle them off and cause them to associate being on that surface with the sound. Just ensure you aren't using something too loud, and don't use it too close to your cat, as it could potentially damage their ears.

Knocking Things Over

Another rather common behaviour cats exhibit when they climb onto surfaces is their desire to knock things over and onto the floor. This can lead to them making a mess or even damaging some of your more fragile items. This can be incredibly frustrating, and at times, it may seem like your cat is doing it on purpose. Honestly, they could be. One of the reasons cats choose to do this is because they're bored and want to play with something. Or, they may even be trying to get your attention, and they know that being destructive will do the trick. While you likely won't be able to stop the behaviour altogether, there are ways to try and lessen it. If your kitty is knocking things over from boredom, then make sure that they have plenty of different toys in the home. They should have so much other stuff to play with that they won't consider making fragile items on high shelves their play toys. Also, make sure you are introducing new toys to your cat so they don't grow tired of the same old mundane toys they already have. If they're trying to get your attention, make sure that you're meeting all the basic needs of your kitty. Keep their food and water bowls filled and ensure that you're engaging with them in both active playtime and frequent cuddle sessions. If you're too busy to play with them at that moment, try to temporarily redirect their attention using their toys until you're able to engage in more active playtime. When all else fails, you may have to move your more fragile items into places that your cat can't access. This will prevent them from the temptation, and even the ability, to knock your precious objects onto the floor.

Litter Box Avoidance

Finding that your cat is not using their litter box can be one of the most frustrating behaviours that your cat may display. But good news! There are a few rather easy steps to take to help avoid the behaviour in the first place. For starters, ensure that your cat's litter box is cleaned regularly. This includes scooping it and cleaning the litter daily as well as washing the box out weekly. You also want to make sure you have litter and a litter box that doesn't bother your cat. Some cats are pickier than others, so this may take a bit of trial and error. If you have multiple cats in your house, ensure that you have enough litter boxes for each cat. This ensures that there are plenty of places for your cats to go. If they suddenly start avoiding the litter box, it could be a sign that something is medically wrong. If there are no external factors that could have triggered it and you've ruled out any other potential stressor, then you should take your cat in to get checked out for a clean bill of health at the vet.

Difficult Sleep Schedule

Many cat owners complain of their cats keeping them up at night. This is especially true for newly adopted ones and kittens, who are still adjusting to your schedule. As we've discussed in length, feline behaviour dictates their sleep schedule. They tend to be awake and most active around dawn and dusk while sleeping intervals throughout the day and night. Because of this, it can be difficult to get your cat to sleep at the same time as you do. It may even become near impossible to sleep with your cat, which can be disappointing as that's one of the best parts of owning a pet.

You won't be able to completely change this behaviour or train it out of them in the way you can with other quirks. After all, their time awake is entirely dictated by their inner clock. However, there are ways that you can help to curb this behaviour. A tired kitty is the best way to go about this. Ensure that you are playing with them throughout the day so they get out plenty of energy. You can also dedicate a specific play time closer to bedtime to help wear them out. Alternatively, setting up things such as timed feeders or toys could help keep them busy and distracted while they're awake during the night. That way, they won't bother you as much and you can get some sleep. Thankfully, your cat can and will adjust more to your schedule with time.

Along the same line, you may find that your cat wakes you up far too early. Perhaps they're eager for breakfast or looking for some attention and playtime. No matter what they're hoping for, it can be especially frustrating on those mornings that you're hoping to get some extra sleep. Once again, this habit is influenced by their instincts. Cats are typically awake that early to eat, so some of the best ways to alter this habit are through food.

As we discussed in Chapter six, some of the best ways to feed your kitty are through timed feeders or free feeding. Using both of these can keep them from bothering you so early. If you've elected not to use either of these, or they still seem to want you awake at dawn, you can use treats to help alter this. Start by setting a timer shortly before the time that your cat will typically try to wake you up. Give your cat a treat, which can be any kind that they like.

Over time, start moving the alarm a few minutes later while still giving them the treat whenever the alarm goes off. By the time that the alarm is set to the exact time you want to wake up, they will start to associate the timer with the treat, making them less inclined to bother you earlier in the morning.

General Do's and Don'ts

No matter what behaviour you are trying to train into (or out of) your cat, there are a few methods and pointers to keep in mind. Following these general tips will make training a bit of an easier process and will likely cause you significantly less stress.

It is far more effective to encourage positive behaviours in your cat rather than punishing negative ones. While the negative association is very possible and can sometimes be used in certain training methods, they tend to be more receptive to positive associations. So it's much more effective to reward your pet when they exhibit the behaviour that you are wanting. When you notice that your cat is using their scratching post, or they halt a behaviour you're trying to stop, reward them with a treat or even give them a pet or a scratch. They'll associate the positive behaviour with treats and affection and will be encouraged to do it more.

Another general training method is focusing on redirecting your cat rather than fussing at them or punishing them. If you notice that your cat is doing something that you want them to stop, such as scratching up your furniture or jumping onto your counters, try redirecting their attention to something else. You can use a toy to distract the cat from them or simply remove the kitty and place them elsewhere. The point is to try and redirect their attention, focus, and energy on something that they are allowed to do. This action attempts to cause the loss of the desire to continue with the negative behaviour.

Give them an equivalent for what they are looking to do. Do they keep getting up on a high counter? Place them on their cat tree instead. Do they keep scratching up the couch? Direct them to their scratching post. They keep playing with your hands or items that you don't want them chewing on? Give them one of their toys or have a short play session with an acceptable object. You want to show them that their behaviour isn't necessarily *wrong*, it's just in the wrong place or with the wrong things.

That aside, here are a few things and training methods that you definitely want to avoid for the wellbeing and safety of your cat. You should not verbally or physically try to reprimand or punish your cat. While this action may stop them at the moment, it does not effectively train the behaviour out of them. Hitting or yelling at your pet will only succeed in making them stressed and potentially fearful of you. This, in turn, can cause them to misbehave even more or even turn aggressive toward you and other people. There are a lot of ways to successfully train a cat, so never resort to hostility. There may be moments when you get frustrated or angry, especially if your cat has damaged something expensive, but it's important to take a moment to calm down before using a more effective training method, rather than just lashing out immediately with anger. You should also avoid leaving things scented, with smells that cats dislike, sitting around as a method of deterrent. Many scents that cats dislike are actually because those things are dangerous and toxic to them.

Clicker Training

Clicker training is a popular method often used to train dogs, but did you know that you can do this with your cats as well? Repetitive positive associations cause this method to be a very effective way to redirect them. The reason that it works so well for felines is due to their receptiveness to this type of association. It is effective in training cats to even do tricks, but it can also be used to correct their misbehaviours. When choosing a clicker to use, you don't have to have an actual clicker. While there are some designed specifically for cats, they aren't necessary for the method to be effective. You could make a clicking sound with your tongue, use a single syllable word, or you can even find something else that makes a clicking noise. However, you shouldn't use a normal clicker, such as one designed for dogs, as they can be loud and startling for your cat.

To begin the training, you will need to get some treats that your cat loves. This can be store-bought treats, bits of fish, or their favorite snack—Any little treat will do. The process begins with a positive association. Sit down with your cat at varying increments of time: This is to ensure that they don't necessarily associate the treats with the time of day but instead connect it to the sound. Click your clicker, or use the other method you may have decided on, and immediately hand your cat a treat. Repeat this until you notice you have lost the attention of your pet.

Try to have these small sessions each day. Over time, they will begin to associate the noise with the treat. Once you notice they have, you can begin using the noise to train them!

When it comes to using this method to correct their misbehaviours, you will need to pair the clicker tool alongside your chosen deterrents. Using one of the methods to deter your cat, which we have covered extensively earlier in this chapter, will still help to discourage their incorrect behaviours. But if your cat is showing the correct behaviour, such as using their scratching posts or climbing their cat tower instead of on your countertops, the clicker method will help encourage them to keep repeating this action. Whenever you notice them doing what you want them to do, use the clicker and follow with giving them a treat. They will associate the behaviour that you are encouraging with the treats and the sound of the clicker. Then your cat will be inclined to continue doing it because they want to be rewarded.

Conclusion

All things considered, cats may seem like complex creatures, but they're not too difficult to read once you break down their behaviour. All you need to do is take a step back and attempt to understand things from a more cat-like perspective. If you appreciate how they look at and understand the world, you can start to see why cats behave the way they do. Despite now living comfortably in our homes, they were never really domesticated the way dogs and other animals were. With a significant lack of selective breeding and human intervention, the domestic cats we know today remain closely related to their genetic ancestors and natural wild behaviour. Remember: This has a significant influence on many of their typical habits.

For the most part, cats don't seem all that expressive, but you just have to know what to look for and when to pay attention. Their body language paired with their various vocalizations will easily clue you in on how they are feeling. Just ensure that you take in the whole picture and not just focus on specific aspects. Recognizing the habits and interactions of cats will also help you determine what's normal behaviour and what isn't. You'll easily know when they are happy and comfortable or when something is wrong.

The first thing to remember is, despite not feeling the same complex feelings that we do, they still experience a range of positive and negative emotions. They even use those to express their affections toward their owners. Cats are typically solitary by nature and don't necessarily rely on their owners for companionship, but they seem to enjoy it. Regardless of their reputation for being aloof, they recognise and form deep connections with their human friends—Often looking to them for social cues and reassurance. It should give you some confidence to know that your cat does love and trust you, even if they don't express it as clearly as you wish they would!

By and large, a cats' sense of smell is one of their most important and is one of their sharpest. It helps them to determine information about their environment, other animals around them, and even the safety of some plants and other objects they may find. Smell also plays a rather important role in forming their territory. It deters others from the lands they roam on: The smell of neighboring cats helps indicate which places they can safely travel. Some cats may live in colonies or groups under certain conditions. Although they tend to be solitary by nature, their decision heavily depends on personal preference and personality. While this plays a major role in their life as strays, this can also have an impact on them at home if you decide to bring another cat or even a dog into their environment. Remember to decide on this based on your cat's personality and likelihood to accept them—and if you do, introduce them slowly and safely so that both remain comfortable. You wouldn't want a new roommate in your space without so much as an introduction, would you? So, why would your pet?

As has been noted, cats are rather different from humans, and other animals. However, their diets and habits concerning them are just as important. Knowing what normal eating and drinking mannerisms look like can help ensure your pet is getting plenty of food and water. Determining the best way to do so should be dependent on what is most normal. Don't forget to ask yourself: Is this healthy and natural for them, while still also being their personal preference? If the answer is yes, then great! This also goes for cat sleeping patterns, which can vary significantly from ours. A kitty who sleeps all day is not a lazy one, but one who is just conserving energy for their hunting time!

In essence, even if their normal behaviours are an instinct to them, it's still important that cats are properly trained. You won't stop them entirely, but if you can master redirection, it will save both of you frustration. It will take time and patience, but what training doesn't? It'll be worth it in the end. And both you and your kitty will be happier! Then you can show your well-trained pet off to those that claim cats can't be taught anything.

To summarize, always keep in mind that no matter how hard you study cat behaviour, the best way to get to know your own is to spend time with them. They are complex animals with their own vastly different personalities and even personal tastes. The more time you devote to playing with, cuddling, and being around your kitty, the better you can read your cat's behaviour—especially with the information from this book! Besides, how else will you get to see their cute antics?

Ultimately, it doesn't matter what kind of pet you own, your priority should always be providing the best environment for them. Of course, that includes cats! Despite their reputation as being more independent and lower maintenance than dogs, they need more than just basic necessities to have a truly healthy environment. They deserve to have a properly structured place to live so that they can thrive.

With this closer bond you formed with your kitty, and the knowledge you have gained from this book, you should be able to create an enriching home for them. After all, if your cat is content and confident, then you will be too!

References

Adams, C. (2021, March 12). *10 smells that cats love.* Excited Cats. https://excitedcats.com/smells-that-cats-love/

Bailey, A. (2018, March 7). *Why do cats knock things over? 3 reasons and how to stop the behaviour.* Catster. https://www.catster.com/cat-behaviour/why-do-cats-knock-things-over

Boicelli, C. (2020, June 15). *Keeping your cat out of your houseplants.* Preventative Vet. https://www.preventivevet.com/cats/how-to-keep-your-cats-out-of-your-houseplants

Bourquin, B. (2021, May 10). *How to train a cat to stop doing almost anything.* WikiHow. https://www.wikihow.com/Train-a-Cat-to-Stop-Doing-Almost-Anything

Bowen, J. (2018, December 12). *Feeding behaviour in cats.* Vetfocus.royalcanin.com. https://vetfocus.royalcanin.com/en/scientific/feeding-behaviour-in-cats

Breeze, A. (2020, January 30). *10 smells that attract cats.* Animalwised.com. https://www.animalwised.com/10-smells-that-attract-cats-2434.html

Buzhardt, L. (n.d.). *Why do cats have whiskers?* Vca_corporate. https://vcahospitals.com/know-your-pet/why-do-cats-have-whiskers

Cat sleeping habits. (2021, March 26). Sleep.org. https://www.sleep.org/cats-sleep-habits/

The cat's meow: Understanding feline language. (n.d.). The Humane Society of the United States. https://www.humanesociety.org/resources/cats-meow

CCSPCA. (2019, April 22). *Is bathing a cat really necessary (or just a myth in caring for pets)?* Central California SPCA, Fresno, CA. https://www.ccspca.com/blog-spca/education/bathing-a-cat/

Duno, S. (2014, March 18). *12 sounds cats make and what they mean.* Modern Cat. https://moderncat.com/articles/12-sounds-cats-make-and-what-they-mean/

Four ways to stop a cat biting and scratching. (n.d.). Animal Friends Pet Insurance. Retrieved October 12, 2021, from https://www.animalfriends.co.uk/pet-advice/cat/cat-training-behaviour/four-ways-to-stop-a-cat-biting-and-scratching/

Freeport Veterinary Hospital. (2019, March 25). *Creating a harmonious multi-cat family.* Freeport Veterinary

Hospital.
https://www.freeportvet.com/services/cats/blog/c
reating-harmonious-multi-cat-family

Gerrity, S. (2020, September 8). *How to train your cat using a clicker.* Daily Paws. https://www.dailypaws.com/cats-kittens/cat-training/clicker-training-for-cats

Handl, S., & Fritz, J. (2018, December 12). *The water requirements and drinking habits of cats.* Vetfocus.royalcanin.com. https://vetfocus.royalcanin.com/en/scientific/the-water-requirements-and-drinking-habits-of-cats

How cats and dogs communicate. (2014, October 14). Rover-Time. https://www.rover-time.com/how-cats-and-dogs-communicate/

How do cats see human faces? (n.d.). Petfinder. https://www.petfinder.com/cats/cat-behaviour-and-training/how-cats-see-human-faces/

Howard, B., & 2020. (2020, October 22). *Do cats dream when they sleep?* Daily Paws. https://www.dailypaws.com/cats-kittens/behaviour/cat-psychology/do-cats-dream-when-they-sleep

Howard, K. (2018, December 19). *Can cats sense our emotions?* Cuteness.com.

https://www.cuteness.com/13715715/can-cats-sense-our-emotions

Ingraham, L. (2021, August 31). *Why do cats perch?* WagWalking. https://wagwalking.com/behaviour/why-do-cats-perch

Intelligent Cat Care Blog. (2019, January 15). *Understanding the hunting behaviour of pet cats: An introduction.* Icatcare.org. https://icatcare.org/understanding-the-hunting-behaviour-of-pet-cats-an-introduction/

International Cat Care. (2018a, October 5). *The origins of cats.* Icatcare.org. https://icatcare.org/advice/the-origins-of-cats/

International Cat Care. (2018b, October 5). *The social structure of cat life.* Icatcare.org. https://icatcare.org/advice/the-social-structure-of-cat-life/

Is your cat drinking enough water? (n.d.). Www.cats.org.uk. Retrieved October 12, 2021, from https://www.cats.org.uk/northherts/feature-pages/is-your-cat-drinking-enough-water

Jackson, S. (2019, September 23). *Cats really do need their humans, even if they don't show it.* NBC News; NBC News. https://www.nbcnews.com/health/health-

news/cats-really-do-need-their-humans-even-if-
they-don-n1057431

King, I. (2015, January 7). *Why cats thrive on routine.* The
Conscious   Cat.
https://consciouscat.net/2015/01/07/cats-thrive-
routine/

Krouse, L. (2021, July 3). *What smells do cats hate?* Great
Pet   Care.   https://www.greatpetcare.com/cat-
behaviour/what-smells-do-cats-hate/

Lam, J. (2017, April 11). *Can your cat cohabitate with other
small   animals?* The   Honest   Kitchen   Blog.
https://www.thehonestkitchen.com/blog/can-
your-cat-cohabitate-with-other-small-animals/

Libal, A. (n.d.). *Do cats dislike the smell of mint?* The Nest.
Retrieved   October   28,   2021,   from
https://pets.thenest.com/cats-dislike-smell-mint-
10432.html

Lichtenberg, D. (2012, January 25). *How to keep the peace
in   a   multi-cat   household.*
Https://Www.petful.com/.
https://www.petful.com/pet-health/multi-cat-
household-tips/

Litter Robot Blog. (2019, May 21). *Are any essential oils
safe for cats?* Litter-Robot Blog. https://www.litter-
robot.com/blog/2019/05/21/essential-oils-safe-
for-cats/

Litter Robot Blog. (2020, March 23). *Surprising smells cats hate.* Litter-Robot Blog. https://www.litter-robot.com/blog/2020/03/23/smells-cats-hate/

Litter Robot Blog. (2021, April 2). *Do cats and ferrets get along?* Litter-Robot Blog. https://www.litter-robot.com/blog/2021/04/02/do-cats-and-ferrets-get-along/

Llera, R., & Buzhardt, L. (n.d.). *Why cats sniff rear ends.* Vca_corporate. https://vcahospitals.com/know-your-pet/why-cats-sniff-butts

Marc-André. (2019, December 8). *How to safely care for both fish and cats in the same home.* Katzenworld. https://katzenworld.co.uk/2019/12/08/how-to-safely-care-for-both-fish-and-cats-in-the-same-home/

Murphy, S. (2015, May 1). *Tips to living with cats and small pets harmoniously.* The Honest Kitchen Blog. https://www.thehonestkitchen.com/blog/tips-to-living-with-cats-and-small-pets/

Parker, H. (2009). *Cats and compulsive scratching, licking, and chewing.* WebMD. https://pets.webmd.com/cats/guide/cats-and-compulsive-scratching-licking-and-chewing#1

PetMD Editorial. (2011, December 14). *Why do cats sleep so much?* Petmd.com.

https://www.petmd.com/cat/behaviour/evr_ct_w hy_do_cats_sleep_so_much

PetMD Editorial. (2017, April 21). *9 common cat behaviour problems (and how to fix them).* Www.petmd.com. https://www.petmd.com/cat/slideshows/9-common-cat-behaviour-problems-and-how-fix-them#slide-1

PetMD Editorial. (2018, January 19). *5 unusual cat eating habits.* Petmd.com. https://www.petmd.com/cat/nutrition/5-unusual-cat-eating-habits

PetMD Editorial. (2020, January 23). *Why do cats knead?* Petmd.com. https://www.petmd.com/cat/behaviour/evr_ct_w hy_do_cats_knead

Petplan. (2017, December 12). *Understanding cats' emotions – do cats have feelings for their owners?* Www.petplan.co.uk. https://www.petplan.co.uk/pet-information/cat/advice/understanding-cats-emotions/

Purina. (n.d.). *Do cats always land on their feet?* Www.purina.co.uk. https://www.purina.co.uk/articles/cats/behaviour/common-questions/do-cats-land-on-their-feet

Rough play in a kitten or adult cat. (2018, February 16). HSHV. https://www.hshv.org/rough-kitten-play/

Science Reference Section, Library of Congress. (2019, November 19). *How did cats become domesticated?* The Library of Congress. https://www.loc.gov/everyday-mysteries/item/how-did-cats-become-domesticated/

Shojai, A. (2019a, August 22). *How cats show they love you.* The Spruce Pets. https://www.thesprucepets.com/how-cats-show-love-553978

Shojai, A. (2019b, October 25). *Why cats smell everything.* The Spruce Pets. https://www.thesprucepets.com/cat-communication-by-smell-553941

Shojai, A. (2021, April 29). *Understanding why cats groom themselves.* The Spruce Pets. https://www.thesprucepets.com/understanding-cat-grooming-553960

Summons, D. (n.d.). *How does a cat land on its legs when dropped?* Www.physlink.com. Retrieved November 24, 2021, from https://www.physlink.com/education/askexperts/ae411.cfm

Sung, W. (2015, July 29). *Why does my cat... like to pounce on me?* Vetstreet. http://www.vetstreet.com/our-pet-experts/why-does-my-cat-like-to-pounce-on-me#:~:text=The%20most%20common%20reasons%20cats

Sung, W. (2018, October 11). *Cat language 101: How do cats talk to each other?* Www.petmd.com. https://www.petmd.com/news/view/cat-language-101-how-do-cats-talk-each-other-37620

Syufy, F. (2021, March 9). *How to stop destructive chewing in cats.* The Spruce Pets. https://www.thesprucepets.com/destructive-chewing-by-cats-551790

Tuft and Paw. (n.d.). *The definitive guide to cat behaviour and body language.* Tuft + Paw. https://www.tuftandpaw.com/blogs/cat-guides/the-definitive-guide-to-cat-behaviour-and-body-language

Turner, J. (2020, October 19). *10 smells that cats hate.* Animalwised.com. https://www.animalwised.com/10-smells-that-cats-hate-672.html

Vecsi, E. (2019, April 18). *Understanding the art of cat pouncing.* Catster. https://www.catster.com/cat-behaviour/the-art-of-cat-pouncing

Village Veterinary Clinic. (2021, July 13). *The secret to navigating a multi-cat household.* Village Veterinary Clinic. https://www.villageveterinaryclinic.com/services/cats/blog/secret-navigating-multi-cat-household

Virbac. (2016, July 19). *Do cats hear better than dogs?* Us.virbac.com. https://us.virbac.com/home/resources/blog/pagecontent/the-buzz-and-bark-from-virbac/do-cats-hear-better-than-dogs

WebMD. (2020). *Tips for how to bathe your cat or kitten.* WebMD; WebMD. https://pets.webmd.com/cats/bathing-your-cat#1

WebMD Veterinary Reference. (2021). *Why do cats purr?* WebMD. https://pets.webmd.com/cats/why-do-cats-purr

Why do cats like small spaces? (2020, March 30). Feltcave. https://feltcave.com/blogs/cat-beds/why-do-cats-like-small-spaces

Your cat's world: How your feline uses his senses. (2016, December 7). Hartz. https://www.hartz.com/your-cats-world-how-your-feline-uses-his-senses/

Printed in Great Britain
by Amazon

49779833R00079